The 25th Hour

Neal Schore

How to Thrive

(And Gain Ridiculous Amounts of Time)

By Getting Out of Your Own Way

GALLERY BOOKS UK

London · New York · Amsterdam/Antwerp · Sydney/Melbourne · Toronto · New Delhi

First published in the United States by Avid Reader Press, an imprint of Simon & Schuster, LLC, 2026

First published in Great Britain by Gallery Books, an imprint of Simon & Schuster UK Ltd, 2026

1 3 5 7 9 10 8 6 4 2

Simon & Schuster UK Ltd
7th Floor
199 Bishopsgate
London
EC2M 3TY

www.simonandschuster.co.uk
www.simonandschuster.com.au
www.simonandschuster.co.in

Simon & Schuster Australia, Sydney
Simon & Schuster India, New Delhi

The authorised representative in the EEA is Simon & Schuster Netherlands BV, Herculesplein 96, 3584 AA Utrecht, Netherlands. info@simonandschuster.nl

A CIP catalogue record for this book is available from the British Library

Trade Paperback ISBN: 978-1-3985-5099-5
eBook ISBN: 978-1-3985-5100-8

Interior design by Ruth Lee-Mui

Printed and Bound in the UK using 100% Renewable Electricity at CPI Group (UK) Ltd

FSC www.fsc.org MIX Paper | Supporting responsible forestry FSC® C013604

"*The 25th Hour* offers a refreshing take on productivity. Neal Schore makes a compelling case that we don't lose time to tasks – we lose it to our reactions. By learning to manage the emotions that drive our behaviour, we can reclaim focus, improve our relationships and ultimately get more out of every day"
Nir Eyal, bestselling author of *Beyond Belief, Indistractable* and *Hooked*

"*The 25th Hour* is both a revelation and a challenge. Schore redefines mediocrity not as incompetence but as cowardice – the idea you didn't share, the tough conversation you sidestepped, the decision you let drift. The result is a bracing guide to reclaiming your time by confronting the emotional habits that quietly give it away"
Daniel H. Pink, #1 *New York Times* bestselling author of *Drive* and *The Power of Regret*

"This essential guide shows why all management is really self-management, and how mastering yourself is the fastest way to stop wasting time and start getting what matters done. In *The 25th Hour,* Neal Schore unfurls life-changing tools that will change how you think, work and lead"
Leslie John, author of *Revealing*

"Here is a book with a life-changing message: we spend too much time managing the wrong things. If we want a workplace that is more creative and productive, we need to learn how to manage ourselves. Not only will everyone around you be happier, less stressed and have more time – so will you!"
Kamini Lane, President & CEO, Coldwell Banker Realty

"*The 25th Hour* speaks to the high achievers who have optimised everything except their own emotional reactions. Neal Schore offers a surprisingly fun playbook for reclaiming the hours you didn't realise you were losing"
Dan Heath, *New York Times* bestselling author of *Reset*

Contents

Contents

Author's Note

This book presents stories from my clients and others to illustrate conceptual points and usage of my coaching tools. I've changed names and identifying details in most cases to maintain privacy, but I've otherwise tried to present these stories as accurately as possible.

Introduction

For several years, Ken oversaw a technical team charged with designing a very complicated new product for a highly visible client. Despite his best efforts, an initial live test of the product failed. It sucks, but it happens. Yet he couldn't seem to shake it off and move on. He became despondent and preoccupied with negative thoughts. Spending hours alone, he pondered his shortcomings and missteps. Perhaps he was incompetent. Perhaps he hadn't hired the right team. Perhaps he was out of his league as a leader. Perhaps he would now be out of a job. Perhaps, perhaps, perhaps.

After about ten days, he realized that he wasn't managing himself very well and was squandering precious time. He needed to do a reset by reining in his fear response. Reaching into the set of tools that we'd worked on together, he pulled out one called "What's the Worst Thing That Can Happen?"

I often teach this device to clients, young professionals, students and friends. Here's how it works: if you're wasting time worrying, you need to sit down, take a pause, and force yourself to review methodically all the biggest, scariest things that could possibly happen in your present situation. After taking five to ten minutes to make a list, you consider the items one by one and evaluate how likely they are to *actually* occur. You specify the probability that each bad outcome could happen: is there a 2, 5 or 10 per cent chance? Twenty per cent?

Most people quickly realize that their worst-case scenarios have a vanishingly small chance of happening and that they're spending a crazy amount of time and energy worrying about them. As their fears subside, they stop spiralling, and they become productive again. With a little practice, they can run through this exercise in just a couple of minutes.

When Ken pondered the worst things that could happen, he realized that there was less than a 1 per cent chance that he'd be fired. Sure, he'd have to make some adjustments to his team and its operations – they'd need to internalize what they'd learned from the failure and take appropriate actions. But he was safe from his scary thoughts about losing his job and the embarrassment and instability he would suffer. His team would get a second chance to test the product and probably even a third. Recognizing that helped him stop obsessing and move back into action mode. Soon his team was refocused on revamping the product. His spiralling had cost him ten days, but it could have been much worse.

So many of us operate inefficiently because we fall prey to waves of fear and other negative feelings. We don't know how to manage our emotional responses properly as we encounter situations and interact with others, so we feel anxious, depleted and upset, wondering where all our time has gone. Our relationships deteriorate. We make poor decisions. And all too often, we fail to achieve our goals.

Consider your own life. What *really* causes you to blow through so much time? Is it those countless "cover your butt" emails you send every day? Or is it the unexamined anxiety that, if you're honest, propels you to write so many of them? Likewise, is it the frequent conflicts you have with colleagues? Or is it the emotional swirling on your part that *invites* and then sustains that unproductive drama?

The 25th Hour is a handbook for identifying, recognizing, accepting and managing unhelpful emotional responses. The book teaches you how to turn down the volume on your distracting thoughts and feelings, so that you can get *way* more done in less time. As people who use my approach tell me, they recover so much time that they feel that they've added a 25th hour onto their day. In the process, they turbocharge their careers, while also learning to have fun and laugh a little more. It's pretty amazing.

I've written *The 25th Hour* because our conventional thinking about time management is messed up. Experts often equate saving time with working smarter. As they tell us, it's about cutting unnecessary meetings, sending fewer emails, collaborating more strategically. While tactical adjustments such as these help, they only skim the surface and don't get to the core of time management, which is the ability to handle your underlying behaviour patterns and emotional needs. The essential innovation of *The 25th Hour* is to shift our thinking about time management so that it's not an end in and of itself but rather a pathway to a deeper, more lasting personal transformation. This book, in other words, isn't just about time management; it's about self-*development*.

Unlike other self-development books, which present either general frameworks or tactical advice, I wanted *The 25th Hour* to provide something more useful: a proprietary set of exercises, strategies and tools that will help you manage your professional life better – starting *now*. I've road tested these fun, practical techniques in a wide range of business and personal situations with clients, and they consistently help people get out of their own way, freeing up incredible amounts of time and enabling them to work and live more happily and productively. Again, they gain what seems like a 25th hour in their day.

Inventing the Tools

So who am I and how did I come to understand all of this? Well, I'm not a therapist or academic. I'm more like the coach's coach, the "leader's leader". I'm fortunate enough to be a go-to adviser to some of the most consequential leaders and titans of industry over the past decade or two. My clients hear about me through word of mouth or referral, and they rave about me to *their* colleagues and friends, causing my practice to grow organically. What people really seem to like isn't just my strategies for handling negative emotions and complicated situations in the moment but the lighthearted, nonjudgmental manner in which I work with the tools.

Let me tell you a story – and yes, I'll keep it brief. From a young age, I've had an intuitive and uncanny ability to help others with interpersonal problems and relationships. When I was thirteen, I organized an intervention with my irascible grandmother, coaching her on how to tone down her behaviour, which had become so bad that it was dragging down my parents' marriage. In college, I managed to get onto the national board of my fraternity, where I guided the other board members, who were all wildly successful and decades older than me (read: stick-in-the-muds), to implement major policy changes.

While I was in my twenties, after just two years on the job, I began a fast rise up the ranks at Interep, one of the USA's largest national radio sales and marketing organizations. I became a close, informal adviser to the company's founder and CEO, who again was much older than I was. In my thirties, I made a name for myself as an expert in entrepreneurship, advising several of America's biggest private equity firms and sitting on the boards of notable companies. By the time I was in my forties, I was also running a media and technology company I had founded called Triton Media, which owned Westwood One, one of the country's largest radio networks, as well as Triton Digital, a global technology firm.

As I built my career, I had the honour of becoming an informal coach and mentor to colleagues, business associates and friends. They started coming to me for help, and I offered them practical guidance that led them to improve their relationships, save time and achieve new levels of success. You know that person everyone seeks out when they or someone they know is struggling? For reasons I don't fully understand, that was me. I didn't have anything formal to offer. I wasn't employing some method, framework or philosophy, and I hadn't yet developed my exercises and techniques. I certainly never thought I could make such a big impact helping people to claim back a 25th hour by getting a grip on their emotional responses. I wasn't, in other words, the coach's coach just yet. But my intuition and experiences, apparently, were enough.

I would soon feel inspired to take my practice to the next level. One day during the early 2010s, as I was busy running Triton, my attorney called with a special request. A twentysomething entrepreneur he knew was struggling. "Neal," he said, "you're really good at the development side of leadership. Can you mentor this kid?"

It turned out that "this kid", Mark, had developed a promising app that would solve a problem for a niche audience. But after a year in business, he was totally deflated, having struggled to sign clients, hire staff and raise meaningful money. After chatting with him, I saw that he had the skills, knowledge and vision he needed to succeed. What he lacked was confidence and the ability to focus and soothe himself at difficult times when his fears cropped up. It was a mental self-management problem, eminently fixable so long as he could own up to it.

In offering my assessment, I didn't coddle Mark. I told him what was up in a way that, although direct, was also nonthreatening. "Your issue," I said as we sat in a Chinese restaurant, enjoying our hot-and-sour soup, "is not that you don't have the right team or plan. It's that you're not communicating clearly enough for the staff to understand what you need to accomplish. Also, you're focusing on managing the board and not on productivity. And why is that? Because of one thing: you're afraid of failing."

As the waitress arrived with our main courses, he told me that he knew in his heart that I was right. But then the real magic happened: as we continued to talk, I came up with a simple – some might say obvious – tool he could use to manage himself. He was to write the phrase "I believe in myself" on a piece of paper and tape that onto his computer. As he worked, he would have that phrase staring him in the face as a reminder. It would become his focal point, a mental refuge to which he could return in any uncomfortable or distressing situation. At that moment, something clicked for Mark; he remembers that tool as well as our conversation that day as having been fundamentally life changing.

Mark hired me to coach him on an ongoing basis. As the months passed, I spontaneously created other tools to help him. That first extended coaching gig was fun for me, and it paid off for Mark. He went on to become wildly successful, building his second company into a business with over $100 million in annualized revenue. But honestly, I didn't take my coaching very seriously. I had a big day job building and running Triton, which at the time was generating hundreds of millions of dollars in sales with over seven hundred employees in seven countries.

Over the next few years, I fielded other requests for ongoing, formal coaching. Another friend called and asked me to help a friend in an entirely different industry. That friend in turn told his friend, who wanted help. By 2018, I sat back and realized that without even trying, I was developing a pretty impactful side hustle as a leadership coach. With all of my clients, I had used the same strategies and techniques that I'd developed while helping Mark and his team, continuing to jot down new ones as I developed them. I had amassed a couple of dozen tools, and more were popping into my head every month. I had become more methodical, too, keeping files on my clients and tracking their progress. And I had started to develop a coaching philosophy built around my tools – the notion that we can all save time and operate more productively and efficiently by improving the way we manage our own thinking and behaviour.

I'd noticed a pattern: all of those individuals had the skills, knowledge and attributes they needed to achieve their goals and become formidable leaders at work, at school, or elsewhere in their lives. What they didn't have, regardless of their age or career stage, was the ability to rein in unruly thoughts and emotional responses – a skill that I, too, had lacked earlier in my career but that over time I'd worked hard to cultivate. To a person, they were wasting time stressing about meaningless and unproductive stuff. They were making fear-based decisions. They were letting drama overcome what might otherwise have been well-functioning relationships.

But like me, they didn't need years of therapy to keep their careers and lives on track. All they needed was some easy techniques for cutting through the distractions in the moment, becoming more self-aware, and shifting their mindsets to be more focused and productive. As my clients consistently tell me, mobilizing and mastering my techniques made a profound difference, one that they could measure in terms of time saved, customers added, revenues increased, grades improved and much more.

Becoming Exceptional

Over the past seven years, my coaching practice has blossomed. I now work with both individual clients and executives at companies I advise or help oversee as a board member. My client list has grown to include some of the country's most powerful and promising business leaders. My coaching practice has expanded via word of mouth and without the slightest bit of marketing on my part. Some of my clients are high-profile leaders running massive billion-dollar organizations, while others are young geniuses building the unicorns of tomorrow.

I've been astonished by the results: people find that these self-management tools help them step up and achieve more success – and happiness – by becoming the leaders they've always wanted to be. When a senior partner at a prominent law firm first came to me, he was burned out and on the verge of quitting. After learning and utilizing the tools, he has become dramatically happier and has started killing it with his corporate clients. "I was literally nine toes out the door," he told me, "and now I'm modelling to my partners how to manage our firm without working ourselves to death. I'm spending much more time with my kids, and I'm taking regular vacations for the first time in my career – with my phone turned off. I can't thank you enough!"

A senior leader at a healthcare company told me that I had changed her life by "making it safe to grow professionally and have fun with the tools. I used to behave like an overbearing 'mama bear' in our company, which ate up my time and caused my colleagues to distrust me. Now, I just got promoted to chief operating officer, and I work with focus and precision, pinpointing the tasks I want my team members to do and then letting them do it. Even with a bigger job, I have far more time to help out at my kids' school and take care of my elderly parents."

I'm not giving myself all the credit by any means, but I've seen formerly struggling clients go on to get their shit together and create billions of dollars' worth of value by learning, practising and understanding the tools I've provided them. They've built relationships, saved or started fulfilling careers, and earned promotions galore. All because they've been able to operate more effectively, claim back that 25th hour, and devote it to achieving their goals.

In essence, my strategies work by taking the complicated parts of our professional lives and simplifying them so that we can accomplish more in much less time while enjoying our efforts. What I find interesting, too, about these tools is that they're *cumulative*. As you learn more of them and start using them, and as you become expert in applying them at both work and home, you can combine them with one another to quickly catch yourself from going down familiar rabbit holes or from making misguided, fear-based decisions that will only cost you time and energy to unravel later. By mobilizing these techniques over an extended period, you will learn to master your feelings so that you can interact more productively with others, work more joyfully, and achieve breakout success in your career and life.

Ultimately, you will take on what I call an "Exceptional" mindset. Most of us are trained from birth to behave in Ordinary ways. We instinctively copy what others around us do, adopting what most people would consider the typical behaviour or action in most situations. Such typical behaviour can help us, but more often we're acting at cross-purposes with ourselves out of fear or some other negative emotion. Even when we sense that our rote copying of others isn't serving us, we usually stick with it because we're afraid to take a risk and deviate from the status quo; that's the last thing we'd want to do.

But is it really? The vast majority of people – the Ordinary ones – are poor managers of their professional lives. They waste untold amounts of time and limit their prospects by remaining at the mercy of their patterns and behaving in defensive, fear-based ways. Why would we want to be Ordinary? To have an Exceptional mindset is to become ever more aware of our emotions, managing them well in the moment, avoiding fear-based responses, and behaving in unexpected and counterintuitive ways that truly reflect our values and advance our goals. Exceptional action does involve a certain amount of risk, but it's self-empowering in that it allows us to break our ingrained patterns and let our individuality shine through. Ordinary action, by contrast, is self-limiting, leaving us stuck and swirling. Screw Ordinary – an Exceptional mindset is where it's at!

We might think that senior leaders, by virtue of their experience and level of responsibility, would naturally adopt an Exceptional mindset, but that's not always the case. I've worked with many middle managers who have become so adept at handling their emotions and fears that they behave in admirably Exceptional ways, even more than the top executives of their organizations do. Displaying Exceptional leadership skills, these middle managers save massive amounts of time, gain the respect of their peers, and position themselves to rise up in their organizations, if that's their ambition.

Likewise, I've met powerful CEOs who, sadly, are all too Ordinary. They're clueless about their professional fears and hapless at managing their behaviour. They might be successful thanks to luck or their inborn talents and personalities, but their inability to take control and wrench themselves away from an Ordinary mentality prevents them from maximizing their potential and achieving a joyful success. The tools in this book will help you, regardless of your rank, title or age, to achieve a 25th hour – and frankly, have more fun – by breaking free of an Ordinary mindset and becoming proudly, joyfully Exceptional.

A Different Kind of Time Management

I once had an encounter with a client named Stephen who was the chief technology officer at a fast-growth company. On the surface, he seemed cool, calm and sophisticated, but he had a nasty case of impostor syndrome. Having served in the military, he'd had it drilled into his brain that he needed to defer to the leaders above him – a behaviour that was *very* Ordinary. Now, in civilian life, he struggled to break that pattern and see himself as a strong, competent leader in his own right.

One weekend, he found himself grappling with a case of the "Ucks". I'm sure you know what this is. You wake up and think, "Uck, I have to go to that meeting." Then, as the day passes, you think, "Uck, I have a client lunch" and "Uck, I've got to call that client" and "Uck, I've got to pick up my kids from school" and so on. In your mind, everything seems heavy – it takes on extra and unnecessary meaning, leading to a storm of negative self-talk. You really start beating yourself up. In this way, you sap your motivation, slowing yourself down and preventing yourself from getting stuff done. You wind up taking way more time than you expected just to do the simplest things.

In this book, I'll show you how to break out of those annoying Ucks and swiftly redirect your focus so that you can preserve time and productivity. Stephen knew quite well how to get rid of the Ucks, but on that particular weekend, they were so bad that he forgot all about his tools. The Ucks led him into a Category 5 hurricane of self-doubt and self-pity: *I don't know what I'm doing. Nothing I'm doing is working. It's pointless. My team hates me. My company is going down the toilet. I'm letting everyone down. I suck at my job. And to make matters worse, my family is pissed at me since I'm so distracted.*

Finally he texted me, and I reminded him to pause, remember his tools, and put them to work.

"Damn," he said, "I wish I'd done that."

"Yep."

"So you mean I've wasted the past forty hours with my mind spinning?"

"You sure have."

I wasn't about to let him off the hook. I reminded him that he now had to pay himself back the time he'd wasted – a tool called "Credits and Debits". Over the next forty days, he would have to use his tools more deliberately to claw back an extra hour per day. A thirty-minute meeting had to become fifteen minutes. A ten-minute phone call had to become two minutes. Not because he was giving those activities short shrift but because he was using the tools to become even more self-aware and cut through even more of the mental noise – both his own and others' – that otherwise would have bogged him down. I'm happy to report that he not only paid himself back the forty hours in less than forty days, but that each credit and debit he logged served as a further reminder to reinforce how to use the tools to avoid the Ucks.

As Stephen's example suggests, I have my clients focus on the time they're saving or wasting in working with the tools. But again, these tools aren't fundamentally about saving time; they're about shifting how you see and interact with people, so that you can manage yourself better and in turn save time, while also improving the quality of your experience. Time management is a helpful way of structuring an ongoing personal growth process. The extra time you earn back becomes a tangible benefit that you can track and that makes you want to master the tools even more. You get that elusive 25th hour – and you become a better, more self-aware person to boot. Plus, it's super fun!

My clients have asked me for years to package this approach into a book that they can give to their teams, other leaders in their companies, friends and even family members. People who've experienced my tools know their value firsthand. They truly believe that their employees would benefit from mastering them, as would employees and managers at many other businesses large and small. At first I was sceptical, believing that much of the success I'd had I owed to the talented individuals with whom I'd been fortunate enough to work. But after so many years of watching these transformations, and after using the tools to overcome my own fears and insecurities, I've come to agree: these strategies are life changing and need to spread far and wide.

I believe that anyone from CEOs to students can use these strategies and techniques in the moment to enhance their self-awareness and break old, entrenched, fear-based patterns, managing their time more efficiently and to significantly better effect. When you incorporate them into your life, you'll start seeing results almost immediately. Stick with them over time, and you'll learn to see past your ingrained thinking, find your authentic power, build trust and confidence, free up ridiculous amounts of time you never thought you'd have, and enjoy your life more.

What would *you* do with an extra hour – or three – in your day? How amazing would your life be if you could finally unshackle your behaviour from your fears?

It's time to find out.

Part I

Life-Changing Tools for Managing Yourself

This section of the book is your 25th hour power pack. In the first two chapters, I'll present fundamental techniques that will allow you to become more effective in everyday situations by managing your own reactions instead of trying to change other people. You'll save all the time you would have spent worrying and engaging in needless conflict. I'll then introduce you, in chapter 3, to additional tools that will help you use time management as a way of deepening the shift toward self-management and becoming Exceptional. You'll start to track your progress and motivate yourself to practise the many other techniques and strategies I'll teach you.

One

The One Question You Can't Forget to Ask

Not long ago, I coached a young CEO named Cara who had raised $75 million in funding to grow her business but felt overwhelmed and stuck. She couldn't seem to stay organized, nor could she exert more control over her busy schedule. When she arrived home at the end of each day, she felt exhausted, but she also wasn't sure what she'd actually accomplished. In Cara's mind, her job as CEO was to tackle big tasks such as crafting strategy, collaborating with the board of directors, and developing key talent. Yet in large part because she didn't trust her management team and insisted on micromanaging many areas of the business, she couldn't seem to get any of that done. Her frustration had become so acute that she started to feel like a fraud and a "fake" CEO.

To help Cara, I reminded her of a foundational tool I teach called "What's the Intent?" This is typically one of the first strategies I teach clients when they begin working with me. I love it because it's extremely simple and enormously powerful. It focuses a conversation, helping you probe beneath the surface of what someone is saying or asking to get to the core. Here's how it works: when someone approaches you and asks a question or makes a statement of any kind, don't respond right away. Instead, pause for a moment and ask yourself, "*Why* is this person telling or asking me this? What's their real intent?"

Imagine you're a manager, and a member of your team reaches out with questions about a project they're working on. They might have substantive business issues that require your help – a problem with a new client, a piece of technology that isn't working. But most of the time what they really want – in the guise of asking a substantive question – is face time with you. Feeling fearful and insecure, they crave recognition and want to cosy up to you and get on your good side. Do you really want to spend thirty unplanned minutes on *that*? Not so much. But by understanding their intent, you can avoid a pointless conversation and dispense with their question in just a few short minutes.

Using "What's the Intent?" is also a powerful way to help soothe your own agitation. Let's say you're a middle manager in a meeting with several senior leaders, and one of them asks you a tough question. It really ticks you off. You might respond defensively and afterward spend hours (or days) fixating on the encounter: *Why were they targeting me like that? Why don't they respect me? Do they think I don't know my shit? Did I say something that suggests I don't know my shit? Who else thinks I don't know my shit? Why did I respond like that?* And on and on it goes.

Now imagine pausing for a moment and considering the person's real intent. You might find that what happened has nothing to do with you. Maybe this leader wanted to look tough in front of their peers. Maybe they were having a bad morning and their question came across more harshly or dismissively than they realized. Maybe they just wanted to be prickly – and you happened to be an easy target. Quickly assessing the person's true intent allows you to respond better in the moment, saving you time you would have wasted on spiralling and feeling angry, fearful or self-conscious.

Back to Cara. She got into the habit of asking "What's the Intent?" and saw an immediate difference. When Bryan, the face time–seeking employee, knocked on her door with a complicated marketing problem that seemingly needed her attention, Cara cued into what was really going on. She deftly sidestepped a long, unscheduled conversation by saying "Hey, Bryan, I understand what you're looking to accomplish with this new campaign. I believe in you and your ability to execute it, and I will support your decision."

Boom.

That conversation, which took all of five minutes, left Bryan feeling more motivated, focused and empowered than he would have had Cara taken a half hour to spell out precisely how she thought he could execute the new campaign. He simply needed some quick reassurance, which was easy for her to give. He left believing that his boss judged him to be capable of making important decisions. As it turned out, he *did* know best what to do. He made some great choices, texting Cara afterward to deliver a brief summary of what he'd done. You can't always be sure that giving an employee more autonomy will lead to a positive result, but happily, it did that time.

Bryan also told his colleagues about the freedom Cara had granted him, which left them feeling more excited about Cara's leadership and energized to perform. And here's the crazy part: as it turned out, Bryan's handling of the new campaign led to a pitch meeting and the closing of an engagement with the largest client in the company's history. Meanwhile, as Cara continued over a period of weeks to off-load such conversations, she got part of her day back that she could now devote to being a "real" CEO. Asking "What's the Intent?" gave her a way to manage not only herself but her team with maturity and focus.

The Angel and the Devil

Let me say a bit more about how "What's the Intent?" works and why this strategy can be so powerful. Our ability to understand the intentions of others around us is fundamental to our lives. If we couldn't read other people's intentions, even the smallest transactions in everyday life would become harder. How would we know that others around us mean to help rather than harm us? We certainly wouldn't be able to work with others on complex collaborative tasks such as serving customers on the front line or coming to consensus about a strategy in a board meeting.

We first learn to read others' intentions as infants, and over time we become pretty darn good at it. As the authors of one scholarly study put it, "Human beings are the world's experts at mind reading. As compared with other species, humans are much more skilful at discerning what others are perceiving, intending, desiring, knowing and believing."[1] Yet our sense of what others intend isn't always as accurate as we might think it is. That's because our biases get in the way, skewing our judgment. If we find someone attractive, for instance, we might think more highly of them in general, and that might influence how we interpret their behaviour. Or we might have what scientists call a "hostile attribution bias", perceiving ambiguous actions as negative or belligerent.[2]

Our insecurities and entrenched assumptions can also distort how we interpret others' actions. To explain why, I need to pause for a moment and take you on a brief tangent, presenting a general concept I use all the time with my clients. I promise it'll be worth it!

Have you ever seen the classic movie *Animal House*? If so, you'll remember a famous scene where one of the characters, a young fraternity brother, is in a morally dicey situation and unsure what to do. A Devil appears on one shoulder, counselling him to commit an improper act. An Angel appears on the other shoulder, telling him to take the higher road. The Devil, as I think of it, is all those voices in our heads that tell us to react defensively, to give in to our habitual responses, to feel fearful and so on. More fundamentally, it's all those self-limiting narratives we tell ourselves about how we *can't* do something, *aren't* talented enough, *won't* succeed at our goals. That's where the Devil gets us! The Angel is our higher self, the part of us that can look at life more objectively and strategically, understand our habitual emotional responses and assumed beliefs, and rise above them to achieve our goals. Listening to the Devil is Ordinary. Heeding the metaphorical Angel is decidedly not.

In many situations, we hear the Devil telling us to respond by feeling bad, lashing out, doubting ourselves and so on. As we learn to use the tools to manage ourselves, the Angel becomes more prominent, but we will still experience tension between our Devil and our Angel. No matter how good we become at managing ourselves, the sneaky Devil still creeps back in from time to time.

I have a client, Bill, who was extraordinarily accomplished, a national leader in his field. At the peak of an illustrious forty-year career, he had successfully run an organization with 140,000 employees. Now that he was retired, he wanted to enjoy a second act as a motivational speaker and consultant. He was hugely confident in most respects, but he found that he tended to become nervous before speeches. When I asked him why, he told me that he was an introvert and not good in front of people.

I found that impossible to believe, so I called bullshit on it. How could a man who had led an organization of 140,000 people possibly be an introvert? Bill explained that when he and his wife had six couples over for a dinner party, he didn't enjoy it. He preferred to dine with just one or two couples. On that basis, he had concluded that he was an introvert.

Again, bullshit! Bill was lying to himself. Just because he didn't like entertaining a huge number of people at his house didn't make him an introvert. He wasn't inwardly focused or bad at interacting with others, nor was he bad at speaking. He was great at it. It was just his Devil cropping up again in his life.

For years, Bill had listened to his Devil without questioning it, leading him to lie to himself about his capacities as a public speaker. His Devil caused him to feel nervous speaking and sensitive if others seemed to question his performance in front of a crowd. If Bill had kept listening to that Devil, he'd have been limiting his prospects of a second career. To succeed, he'd have to neutralize the Devil's power over him by acknowledging his patterned ways of thinking and deciding to part with them.

What form does your Devil take? Until about ten years ago, I'd convinced myself that I was the least creative person alive. I came to believe that because I'm bad at the visual arts. I can't draw a straight line. If you give me a piece of paper and a pen and ask me to draw, it will look as if a kindergartener had done it. Add to that, I don't play a musical instrument, perform in plays, dance or sing. My logical conclusion: I'm not creative. And then one day, a coaching client called bullshit on me.

In the course of emphasizing a point about one of my tools, I remarked that I was the least creative person on the planet. My client laughed out loud at me. When I asked him what was so funny, he said, "Neal, you're lying to yourself."

"No, I'm not."

"You totally are."

My client seemed to be enjoying the chance to coach *me* for a change. Rather than considering the possibility that he was right, I reacted defensively. I went on to offer several examples of how uncreative I was. I was having an Ordinary moment.

My client, to his credit, stood his ground, shooting back numerous examples of metaphors, illustrations and exercises I'd used to support him, including many that appear in this book. "Neal," he said, "nobody else comes up with stuff like that. No joke, you're the most creative person I know. And maybe it's time you owned that."

My mind was officially blown. Wow, I thought, he's right; I *am* creative! I'd been lying to myself for decades, limiting my possibilities. All along, my personal Devil had held me by the neck, and I hadn't even known it.

Ever since that realization, my Devil has been on the back foot. He's still there, but now my personal Angel talks back, telling my Devil, "I'm wildly creative."

What does all this have to do with understanding others' intentions? Well, when we misinterpret someone's actions, we usually haven't thought about what their deeper concerns are, as was the case in Cara's dealings with Bryan. But our inner Devil could also be causing us to *systematically misconstrue* the meaning of others' behaviour. Asking "What's the Intent?" enables us to start a conversation with ourselves about others' behaviour. We test our interpretation of reality and catch our Devil's distortion of it, stopping the Devil in his tracks or, as I like to say, sending our Devil on vacation. Doing so saves us significant time and energy, getting us closer to a 25th hour.

Let's say you're a newly promoted middle manager at a large company. If you feel insecure about your ability to lead a team, which you've never done before, and an employee you're supervising asks a higher-up whether they might leave your team and jump onto another, you might take that as a sign of rejection. In truth, their decision might have had nothing to do with you. Maybe they prefer the projects on which the other team is working. Maybe a good friend of theirs is working on the other team and they'd like a chance to collaborate with them. But the Devil on your shoulder is whispering into your ear, warping your sense of reality.

Your negative impressions cause you to waste time stressing out about your perceived rejection. Worse, they cause you to lash out at your former team member, wrapping you up in pointless drama. You also overcompensate with other team members, concentrating on avoiding additional rejection rather than on helping them to operate efficiently and effectively. Your performance and that of your team lag, acting as a drag on your professional advancement.

Most people don't think to ask about others' intent. They give their Devil free rein, and they fall into the same patterned responses.

They let themselves get bogged down in their own internal swirling, reinforcing their insecurities and preconceived notions in their own minds. It's the Ordinary thing to do – and it costs them.

By asking about intent, you short-circuit this process. With one simple question, you get outside your emotional reactions, redirecting your attention *outward* so that you can better understand others and their concerns. You can identify other motives your employee might have had for requesting a transfer to another team. By realizing that you're likely projecting a whole different meaning onto it, you learn something about yourself – in this case, that you're feeling a little insecure about your new position, perhaps more than you had previously realized. You enable yourself to take control over your own behaviour – to listen to the Angel, not the Devil.

Avoiding Negative Contagion

The real magic of "What's the Intent?" happens when we practise it over time. As we become skilled at stopping to consider intent, we can stop our spiralling more quickly, maximizing our productivity. Again, our Devil never actually goes away, but it does become a shadow of what it once was, its influence over us diminishing. Let me give you an example from my own life.

Have you ever felt slighted or insulted because you heard about a meeting that took place at work and you felt the organizers ought to have invited you? That happened to me recently. A younger executive at a company where I am a very active contributor – I'll call him Mitch – told me during one of our regular updates about a one-hour team meeting he'd recently initiated. Although I didn't let him know it, his decision to exclude me hit me hard, arousing my insecurities: *Why didn't Mitch think to invite me? Does he not respect me? I thought he valued my contribution, but apparently he doesn't.*

Was it something I said? Do I intimidate him? Does he not like being around me?

That line of thinking persisted for about forty-five minutes. I couldn't focus on my work and was pretty useless. I fell into a case of the Ucks. Even reading some benign emails left me irritated. Then I stopped and asked myself: What was Mitch's intent in excluding me? What was going on in his mind?

Stopping to answer those questions led to an immediate adjustment in my thinking. My Ucks vanished. *Of course* Mitch hadn't intended to slight me. And in fact, the situation was quite amusing. I teach senior leaders at his company to increase their productivity by including in meetings only people who will actually contribute. I didn't need to be at that meeting; I had nothing tangible to offer. Had I participated in that meeting, I would have felt frustrated at having wasted an unproductive hour. Confident in his own abilities, Mitch had stayed focused and spared me a courtesy invite. He'd also put himself in a position to shine as the team leader, since I wouldn't be there to distract him or to trigger his Devil. Had I attended, the participants would have directed their attention primarily toward me, not him.

Just a few weeks earlier, I'd done a training session with Mitch and other managers on that very topic. What business did I now have getting upset about not being included? Far from slighting me, Mitch had been following my advice! Instead of expressing my displeasure to him, a move that would have eroded trust between us, I sent him a text applauding him for holding a productive and focused meeting. He got a "cookie" from my Angel (more on this later) instead of feeling my Devil's wrath.

I was thrilled that I hadn't spent hours or days obsessing about having been excluded, as I might have done years ago. I'd only lost forty-five minutes. If I'd found out earlier about the meeting and somehow pressured Mitch to include me in it, my ego might have felt soothed in the moment, but I'd have wasted a full hour sitting through the meeting. Because I'd used "What's the Intent?", I was up fifteen minutes. That realization itself gave me joy and enabled me to regain my focus. Pretty cool!

That was just one interaction. As I continue to ask about intent day after day, my time savings quickly add up. I'm limiting how bogged down in negativity and drama I get, and I'm able to focus on the goals that I care about.

But the true impact of "What's the Intent?" is greater than this. When we feel resentful, angry, jealous or insecure in our relationship with someone at work, these negative emotions become contagious.[3] Others perceive our negativity and mirror it. We ourselves might spread it around. People in workplaces try to handle negative emotions by finding colleagues with whom to commiserate, often under the guise of collaborating with them. We unburden ourselves of our negative feelings and chatter with our coconspirator about what a bad person so-and-so is. How much productive work do we get done during such supposed collaborations? Very little. Worse, our collaborator might go on to gossip to others about how poorly we're being treated.

This dynamic occurs *every day* at companies, so much so that management scholars have a name for those who habitually become coconspirators: they call them "toxic handlers".[4] The amount of time wasted is extraordinary. The executive coach Marshall Goldsmith cites research showing that most employees spend a minimum of ten hours each month venting to their colleagues or serving as a sounding board for others who have become irate.[5] That's a lot of complaining, and each of those employees in turn risks passing their negative vibes on to more people. Left unchecked, the spread of negative emotions can degrade the culture of a workplace, greatly impeding productivity.

By using "What's the Intent?," we prevent ourselves from becoming conduits of negativity. Even better, we can reverse the dynamic and become conduits of positivity. There's a deeper lesson here, one that I'll return to elsewhere in this book. In learning to manage ourselves, we can learn to better manage an entire organization of which we're a part, whether it's a team, a friend group or a company.

Let's say you just got a fantastic new job, and when you deliver the news to Shelley, your best friend, she makes a comment that seems dismissive or unsupportive. You could become upset and toss and turn all night thinking bitter thoughts: *What a jerk! After all I've done for her, she can't be happy for me!* But if you ask yourself why Shelley might have reacted as she did, you might realize that she didn't intend to be a jerk. She's been unhappy with her job, too, and as she just told you a week or two ago, she doesn't believe she has the job prospects that you enjoy. Her true feelings during your latest encounter, if she were to have communicated them, would probably have been along the lines of *I can't stand going in to work. Although ultimately I'm happy for you, I feel really sad that I'm not in the same position. And I'm jealous that you get to have a job you love and I don't.*

Understanding what's going on can shut down your negative spiralling about Shelley, while also triggering your empathy and compassion. Instead of feeling angry, you'll feel concern for your friend and her welfare. The next thought to occur to you might be *What a shame that Shelley isn't feeling good about herself.* You might even feel moved to reach out to her the next day and give her the boost of moral support that she might need and that you wish you'd received. At the very least, you'll understand the need to show sensitivity and refrain from focusing too much on your new job during future conversations with her. Your relationship will take a turn for the better. And since Shelley will feel more supported by you, she might wind up projecting more positivity among others around her.

If we happen to occupy a leadership role, we have a much greater ability to influence others' behaviour for the better. Others are watching us, so our ability to project empathy and compassion in isolated situations such as this can inspire them to behave similarly. We can also choose to institutionalize the practice of asking about intent, turning it into a behavioural norm throughout our organization. It's one thing if an individual starts listening to their Angel rather than their Devil. When an entire group starts to do that, watch out!

My friend Greg, a longtime entrepreneur who has run a series of successful online businesses, has focused his organization on intent. But rather than urging others to ask about intent per se, he has established a cultural norm of *assuming positive intent*. In running meetings, he'll remind people not to go with their initial, negative impression of something a colleague said but instead to cast it in a more positive light. Greg isn't naive; he knows that sometimes people *do* intend to cause harm. If you're getting negative signals from someone, it's important to respond appropriately. But most people are well intentioned, and many of us can be swayed by our own biases to view things in a negative light. By suspending negative judgments and presuming positive intent, we can reap an array of benefits, including considerable time savings.

As Greg has found, presuming positive intent can prove especially helpful when it comes to performance reviews or other situations in which colleagues deliver feedback. "So many people respond reflexively to constructive criticism," he said, "hearing it as 'This person is telling me I did something wrong,' as opposed to 'Oh, this is actually supposed to be helpful to me.'" By presuming positive intent, we can stop ourselves from reacting defensively and hear feedback better. Instead of wasting time perseverating and resenting the colleague who delivered the feedback, we can focus on putting it to work, changing our behaviour and hopefully improving our performance.

As Greg suggested, making a norm of assuming positive intent can have a major impact by helping entire teams avoid drama. He told of one unfortunate situation in which several members of a board were collaborating on an important project. The leader of the project,

Michelle, went to each of her colleagues individually to explain an action she was hoping to take for the organization's benefit and to gain their approval of it. Everyone enthusiastically agreed with her idea, giving her their approval to proceed. But then another board member, upon learning what Michelle was up to, became upset. Approaching each of Michelle's colleagues, he bad-mouthed her approach and questioned her intentions, accusing her of having "gone rogue" and trying to take over the board.

Michelle's actions had been entirely honest and legitimate. But even though the board members had originally agreed with her, they now became suspicious of her motives. Conflict ensued that sucked up valuable time and eroded trust among board members, making them much less effective. If any of those individuals had simply presumed positive intent on Michelle's part, they might have remembered that she'd approached them in a transparent way to gain their approval. But none of them did.

If you take away one tool from this book, please make it "What's the Intent?" It's foundational, and it's so easy to understand and apply. When I teach this strategy to my clients, it usually blows their minds. They've never thought to stop and ponder what others *really* mean by their actions. As they find, doing so yields an immediate impact. Social interactions become less painful, their aftermaths less stressful and mentally taxing. Relationships become stronger. My clients save loads of time they might otherwise have wasted. They become more productive. They enjoy their work more. They put themselves onto a track toward managing their emotions better – toward becoming Exceptional. And they create more positive energy in their teams and organizations. "What's the Intent?" truly is the one question we can't forget to ask ourselves.

Find Your 25th Hour: What's the Intent?

For a week, keep a log of all the professional interactions you had that you found annoying or distracting or that gave you the Ucks. Jot down just enough information to help you reconstruct later what happened.

At week's end, pick three to five of these moments. Replay them in your mind, pausing for a few seconds to try to pin down the other person's intent. Remembering how you responded in the moment, imagine how you *might* have reacted had you understood the other person's intent. Calculate how much time that Exceptional response might have saved you. Pretty significant, right?

Don't judge yourself harshly and become upset. The point is to keep it light and motivate yourself to do better in the week ahead.

Two

How to Stop Yourself from Saying the Wrong Thing

I have three grown sons, and I exposed each of them to my tools from a young age. That's what you do, I guess, when you're the coach's coach. I didn't present the strategies or techniques as "tools" per se; I just sort of wove them into our daily interactions, offering them up to help as problems or challenges arose. I'm sure my advice made me sound like the typical annoying parent. But as my sons have got into their twenties and started their careers, they acknowledge me and find more value in these tools, even using them to claw back a 25th hour.

My oldest son, Jordan, used one of my tools while landing a new job opportunity. Upon starting college, he'd imagined that he'd pursue a legal career. After doing a summer internship at a law firm, however, he'd decided that law wasn't for him. He'd wound up graduating and taking an entry-level position in the entertainment industry – but that, too, wasn't a good fit. In mid-2020, just after the Covid-19 pandemic shut down the business world, he pivoted to focus on a career in real estate investing. Since he had no experience or other background in the industry, he knew he'd have to play catch-up. He was fortunate enough to land a position at a small real estate firm. From there, he joined a private equity firm in the Midwest that specialized in buying and managing apartment complexes.

After a couple of years, he decided to move back to the West Coast to settle down with his wife. As he began interviewing at real estate investment firms there, he realized that his lack of background in the industry was continuing to haunt him, putting him at a disadvantage. Yes, he now understood reasonably well what went into making investments in multifamily housing projects. But many of the firms that were advertising open positions specialized in other niches such as commercial real estate or distressed properties. Other applicants his age had worked at larger firms and had more robust experience and technical knowledge. Jordan found himself in high-pressure interview situations in which potential bosses were testing his technical skills, asking him tough questions to weed him out of contention.

Like most candidates, Jordan did his homework before going into the interviews, thoroughly researching each firm. Still, he had some experience gaps. Instead of panicking and not pursuing potential job opportunities, and instead of wasting time stressing and despairing whether he'd land his ideal job, he whipped out a tool I teach called "Ask Clarifying Questions". It's exactly what it sounds like: in a range of interactions, your best move isn't to say anything substantive but rather to ask the other person to clarify a point. In so doing, you can demonstrate curiosity, give yourself more time to think, and perhaps most important, prompt the other person to engage in more of the talking than you. As we all know, most people love to talk!

Let's say Jordan was interviewing at a firm specializing in commercial real estate investments, and the interviewer asked him about the economic potential of properties that had "second-generation space". Jordan might not have known what "second-generation space" meant. Instead of getting flustered, he answered the interviewer's question by posing one of his own. "I'd love to answer that," he might have said, "but before I do, I'm wondering: How successful have you been with 'second-generation space' investments? Are they a big or growing part of your portfolio?"

Asking a question like this often leads the interviewer to reveal clues to what a term means (in case you're curious, second-generation space is a property where a previous commercial tenant – a restaurant, say – has made improvements, for example installing a commercial kitchen, that a subsequent tenant might be able to use). In that case, Jordan would be in luck: he could adapt in the moment and provide an intelligent answer of his own, one that drew on his technical knowledge while masking his uncertainty about the terminology. He could also use the interviewer's answer as a starting point, elaborating on what the interviewer was saying – a tactic that might enable him to build rapport. At the very least, posing a clarifying question bought him time to devise an answer that sounded more intelligent and thoughtful.

That approach didn't work every time, but it did see him through some tough moments. In those instances, he managed the discussion to showcase his full skill set, enabling interviewers to become more interested in him and less focused on the technical questions. He wound up advancing as a candidate at several top firms before landing a fantastic job.

"Ask Clarifying Questions" is so simple and yet so powerful. You can use it alongside "What's the Intent?" Once you determine a person's intent, ask clarifying questions, often in ways that allow you to make a statement of your own.

Let's return to that situation I described in the introduction to this book – the one where you're a middle manager in a meeting with several executives, and one of them – let's call her Chandra – distracts you and ticks you off by asking a tough question, which initially feels personal. Asking yourself about Chandra's intent prompts you to realize that her actions have little to do with you, thus forestalling perseveration on your part. But how do you respond?

You could say nothing, but that might come across as dismissive or passive-aggressive. You could snap back defensively at Chandra, which is what most people would do. That will likely trigger a protracted discussion and result in some hurt feelings. Either of these options might lead you later to worry (and swirl) about your behaviour and how others perceived it.

Quite often, your best move in a tricky situation is to ask a clarifying question. "Chandra, that's an interesting perspective," you might say. "I'd love to know more about what you're trying to understand so that I can explain." Then stay silent and wait for her answer.

Think of the power of this simple question. What you're really saying is "You're being petty [or distracting or self-serving], and the question you're asking is irrelevant and unhelpful." But you pose this question to Chandra in such a kind, professional way that she is eager to engage with you. Moreover, you put the onus on *her* to answer, and you avoid letting your emotions and habitual patterns prompt a defensive response. Chances are, any individual confronted with a question like this will talk for a while, to the point that they might even forget their initial question. Since you've given Chandra a platform to talk, she'll likely come away respecting you more and thinking of you as more personable. And almost always, you'll contribute toward your 25th hour by avoiding all the back-and-forth clarifying the emotional cleanup.

In this last scenario, posing a clarifying question doesn't necessarily help you figure out the right thing to say, as it did in Jordan's case. It stops you from saying the wrong thing. If you reflect on the encounters you had today, you'll almost certainly find that asking others around you a question about something annoying or distracting they had said would have prevented you from making the situation worse. Just as important, it could have elicited information about the other person, their motivations or their emotional state that you might not have gleaned otherwise. Also, in any conversation, there's no need for you to do all the work. Ask more clarifying questions, and your interactions will be more productive and efficient, with less mental exertion required on your part.

The Power of Curiosity

I've been preaching the gospel of the clarifying question for years now, since I first began coaching. In fact, the tool originated as a way for me to help direct my clients without angering or frustrating them. One of my first clients, a sales leader named Kelly, had a hard time applying "What's the Intent?" to a conflict that was playing out at work. She was so upset about another colleague's behaviour that she couldn't analyse the nuances of their intent very clearly. She was continually obsessing over her *perception* of the colleague's intent and couldn't apply any of her tools to manage her professional situations better. After weeks of examples and illustrations, our conversation was going nowhere, and I was becoming frustrated with her failure to make the simple adjustments required of her. The conflict she was describing seemed silly, a big distraction. By dwelling on it, I felt that she was wasting valuable time. I found myself wondering, *Why does any of this matter?*

I was tempted to blurt out something like "This conversation is senseless", or "I think we're wasting our time here". Instead, out of curiosity, I put it to Kelly: "Why does this situation matter so much to you?"

That question did the trick, instantly shifting our conversation. With Kelly's answer in mind, I moved us toward a more productive dialogue, prompting her to think less about the blow-by-blow of what was happening at work and more about her *feelings* and how they led her to behave. We discovered that the conflict she was having did matter in some sense, because it revealed some underlying fears she was bringing to her professional relationships. Now that we'd surfaced those fears, I could help her consider how to manage herself better. She worked with the tools to address her feelings and change her behaviour, in turn lowering the temperature on the conflict. None of that would have been possible had I just told Kelly that her fixation on the conflict was stupid. By asking a clarifying question, I'd opened up the conversation rather than shutting it down.

I didn't know it at the time, but scientific research confirms that asking questions and adopting a posture of curiosity is a helpful action in relationships. Seeking out information about others – what scientists call "interpersonal curiosity" – can leave people in a relationship feeling more positive and connected.[1] The relationship can seem like a safer place in which to express oneself. Based on studies of romantic relationships, consistently showing curiosity seems to lower the odds of being targeted for an aggressive response.[2]

All of this makes sense: when we take time to ask someone else to explain themselves, we can understand them better and open ourselves to feeling more empathy. They feel more validated and heard. Our listening skills become stronger. The potential for conflict decreases.

Our Ordinary instinct is to respond quickly, and often defensively, without understanding the other person's intent and before posing any clarifying questions. How many times have you been in a conversation only to hear the other person say, "You're not listening to me", "You're not understanding me", or "You just don't get it"? How many times have your conversations become maddeningly circular, with you and your partners or colleagues talking over one another, trying to make a point and then a counterpoint, each of you becoming frustrated and defensive? Such scenarios waste our time and leave us and others stewing for days, weeks and sometimes months. Almost always, someone winds up having to apologize for responding rudely, unprofessionally or unreasonably.

Working with clients, I've often found that asking not one but a series of clarifying questions leads to far more positive outcomes. I once coached two business partners who were struggling to get along. When I say "struggling", I mean they massively distrusted each other and could barely be in the same room without the conversation growing tense. One of the partners felt such overwhelming distrust and anger that the mere mention of the other's name prompted a flurry of angry or bitter comments. He was thinking of leaving the business entirely, even though that would have cost him dearly in financial terms.

My role was to help the partners act more professionally with each other, teaching them tools such as understanding the intent and asking clarifying questions. I also served as a mediator between the partners, hoping to prevent their emotional and distrusting mindsets from destroying the company. Progress was torturously slow. On a weekly basis, seemingly simple business matters would spark a conflict, and I would have to talk one or the other of the partners off a cliff or convince them to be more reasonable. I went into those conversations knowing that I couldn't accuse the partner I happened to be advising of behaving poorly. I needed to model rational behaviour, showcasing how to stay focused and professional so that they could learn to do it themselves. I did so by starting with a basic clarifying question – some version of "Why do you care so much about the issue at hand?" – and working from there.

Let's say that Partner A had decided unilaterally to fire the company's biggest customer because they'd concluded that that piece of business was unprofitable. And let's say that Partner B vehemently disagreed with that decision and asked me to get Partner A to change their mind. When speaking with Partner A, I'd say something such as "I heard that you made a decision to part ways with your biggest customer. I'd love to understand: why would you want to do that?"

Partner A would reply, "I bet you're asking since Partner B told you about it."

Instead of denying it, I'd answer with a question: "I'm genuinely interested to know: why would you think that?"

"Well, I think you're judging me," he'd say.

I'd respond by saying, "Interesting. I'm not judging you or your business acumen. I'm genuinely curious why you'd want to take that action."

Partner A would list any number of reasons. I'd pose follow-up questions to dig deeper. If he said he was "fed up with dealing with the customer", I'd ask him how often he engaged with the client himself. He'd answer in an emotional way, lacking actual data. I'd follow up with similar questions that pushed him to back up his emotional statements with fact. After he struggled to answer several of these questions, Partner A's stubborn posture would finally break. He'd say something such as "You want to know why I'm parting ways with our biggest customer? Because Partner B is tiring me out. I'm exhausted."

I'd respond by saying, "Ahh. I appreciate that candour, and now this makes more sense to me. Thank you for the honesty." I'd then ask why he was exhausted, since he generally has a lot of energy.

In many cases, a line of questioning such as that would lead Partner A to acknowledge that he'd behaved in an Ordinary way – he'd acted reactively, out of emotion, falling prey to his ingrained but unhelpful patterns. That realization allowed us to resolve the dispute while helping us avoid subsequent conflicts. Once we'd clarified a distracting and counterproductive behaviour pattern, Partner A would send me texts proudly announcing that he'd used his tools, focused on the data points that mattered, and behaved in an Exceptional way. Seeking to support that behaviour, I'd ask him to calculate how much time he'd saved himself, his spouse (he frequently complained to her) and his partner. It was, of course, a significant amount.

Sometimes I'd go back to Partner B to probe why he was upset and see if we could use the same tools to make further progress. My curiosity became a magical mediation tool, one that calmed down the partners and allowed us all to gain more information and insight.

Eventually, the partners were able to communicate more civilly with each other and even build some measure of mutual trust and respect. Because they'd stuck it out and managed to work through their issues, they were able to successfully exit the company as they'd long hoped, selling it for a significant sum of money.

Episodes such as those have made "Ask Clarifying Questions" a cornerstone tool of mine. People who've used the tool have seen results across all areas of their lives, not just at work. One of my clients, Ellie, had a daughter in her twenties who was attending nursing school and who had strong beliefs about healthcare issues, especially pertaining to women. Ellie had her own ideas about healthcare policy, and she tried sharing them with her daughter as a way of showing interest in her life and sparking conversation. Unfortunately, her well-intended statements led to arguments, which were stressful for both of them.

Drawing on the coaching I'd given her in her professional life, Ellie stopped making statements and instead began posing questions out of genuine curiosity: What did her daughter think about a particular issue? Why had she come to see it that way? What had influenced her viewpoint? Instead of indulging her motherly urge to talk and advise, Ellie focused more on *listening*. She found that she started to understand her daughter better and that she listened more thoughtfully than she had in the past. Whereas before she had tended to multitask while her daughter expressed herself, now she really tuned in. Conflict between Ellie and her daughter eased, and her daughter became more open, less defensive and more communicative. It was a massive win for them both!

The Curious Leader

People at any age or level of seniority can benefit from asking more clarifying questions, but if you're a senior leader, you *really* need to start doing it. Research suggests that asking questions and showing curiosity is a powerful leadership tool, one that most leaders tend to ignore, perhaps because it's not part of their training. Trial lawyers and reporters learn how to pose questions, but young people taking business courses in college or pursuing their MBAs generally don't. Many people in business think that they and their organizations are more curious than they really are. As one survey found, 83 per cent of senior leaders reported believing that their companies foster curiosity, while just over half of employees agreed.[3]

Two professors at Harvard Business School, Alison Wood Brooks and Leslie K. John, have argued forcefully that leaders would benefit from posing more questions. "Questioning is a uniquely powerful tool for unlocking value in organizations," they wrote. "It spurs learning and the exchange of ideas, it fuels innovation and performance improvement, it builds rapport and trust among team members. And it can mitigate business risk by uncovering unforeseen pitfalls and hazards."[4]

The claim that something as simple as asking a question unlocks economic value might seem excessive, but I can tell you firsthand that it does. At one company where I served as chairman, our team established a training programme for the young analysts the company hires. One day at the office, I passed by a conference room where a group of four new analysts were sitting together. Poking my head in, I made a lighthearted remark about their recent arrival at the company and told them how happy I was to see them. I often do this kind of thing with employees, since I know that engaging personally with the team, especially younger workers, makes a big difference. I was about to continue on my way, but I decided to spend another minute or two with them by asking a clarifying question. "Excuse me," I said, "I'd love to understand what you're doing right now."

The room fell silent. Panic flashed across their faces. Here they were, the newest and most junior members of the team, being questioned by the chairman. After a long pause, one of them shot me an anxious look and said, "Well, I . . . I was a little concerned that I'm not contributing fast enough, so since we're the four newest people, I asked if we could all get together and compare notes about what we've been learning and how we can help one another."

Wow! Most analysts simply plod through the programme, doing what managers tell them. That's Ordinary behaviour. Not those folks; they weren't satisfied with how quickly they were contributing, so they took the initiative and collaborated independently to enhance their development. They were behaving in a distinctly Exceptional way, which was awesome. "I love that you are doing this," I told them. "You all are going to be rock stars."

At a company offsite the following week, I asked those four to stand up in front of the whole company and announced how proud I was that they were taking the initiative, innovating and accelerating their onboarding pace, and getting up to speed by learning from one another. They were floored. I assure you that they will not soon forget that I noticed them and stopped by the conference room that day, let alone showcased them to the entire company.

In that case, asking a clarifying question turned up a valuable and unforeseen opportunity for me to add value as a leader. I rewarded the four analysts for their proactive behaviour, and I held them up as an example for everyone else to follow. If I hadn't asked the question, I wouldn't have understood how great those four analysts were. Nothing terrible would have happened. But nothing good would have happened, either. Over time, our bolder, more innovative culture will create more economic value. Because I'd asked a question, I helped reinforce and advance that kind of culture.

I also saved time, albeit in ways that are difficult to quantify. Many organizations dedicate time and resources to building culture, and that's a good idea. Posing a clarifying question enabled me to do some valuable culture building without having to allot time and resources specifically to that task. I spent a minute chatting with the four analysts and another minute or two recognizing them publicly. The impact of those three minutes on the organization was far greater than if I'd spent a half hour with a PowerPoint deck lecturing people about our desired culture. By posing a clarifying question, I pushed myself further along toward a 25th hour.

There are many kinds of beneficial questions that leaders might ask, but posing a simple, open-ended query such as "I'd love to understand your thoughts" or "I'd love to understand why that matters to you" might be one of the most powerful leadership tactics out there. Reflecting back on my own three decades as a leader, I can't think of a single instance when asking such questions and possibly some similar follow-up queries wasn't productive in some way. The vast majority of the time, it helped surface useful knowledge or insights or prompted someone to articulate a truth about themselves or the organization.

Some Sample Clarifying Queries

- Please help me understand why that concerns you.
- I'm wondering why you're so focused on that project.
- How do you think that person intended for the situation to play out?
- I would love to understand the specific part of the situation that you found offensive.
- How or where do you think you fit into this scenario?
- I would love to understand the exact reason you're distracted.
- In fifteen seconds or less, can you please summarize the main point you're making so I can fully understand it?

Often, asking a clarifying question helps us lead and manage a situation – and save time – because it prompts others around us to offer clues about their intent. It's one thing to wonder internally about a colleague's intent; it can be better to prompt them to reveal it to you, particularly when they come to you upset about something. "It feels to me that this could be an emotional situation for you," you might say. "I would love to know more. Can you please help me understand why this situation is so important to you?"

In responding, they might reveal their intent: "Well, it's not that important – I just want to vent to you about it."

You now know how you can best help, and you avoid wasting time you might have spent giving advice, say, if all they want is someone to listen.

Regardless of where we are in our careers or lives, posing more clarifying questions makes our daily experience easier. Our egos lead us to feel that we must always talk, direct others, tell them what we think. When someone speaks aggressively to us, we become insulted and feel compelled to respond. That takes effort, energy and time. We wind up falling into our own patterns, making the situation more difficult than it needs to be. We can accomplish so much when we pause, prompt someone else to speak, and *listen* to what they're saying. As anyone who has spent time in organizations knows, this is unusual behaviour. But that's all the more reason why you need to do it.

Find Your 25th Hour: Ask Clarifying Questions

This one unfolds over two days. On day 1, go through your time at work as you ordinarily would. Periodically during the day, jot down your quick impressions of the conversations you have, including the time and energy you spent (1) talking and (2) listening and understanding. Note whether you reacted in ways that were Ordinary or Exceptional.

The next day, change it up a bit. Make a practice during each of your conversations of mentally inquiring what the other person's intent might be. As you form a quick hypothesis, ask a clarifying question. Jot down notes about these conversations as you did the previous day, tracking how much time you spent talking and listening and also observing whether you reacted in a way that was Ordinary or Exceptional.

Did you notice any differences? I'm guessing that on day 2 you'll have spent significantly more time listening and less time talking. I also suspect that you'll have reacted more often in ways that were Exceptional. If that's the case, don't stop here. Keep inquiring about intent and asking those clarifying questions!

Three

Time Management as a Pathway to Personal Growth

During one of our sessions, my client Nick told me of an awful charity golf tournament he and his childhood friend Tommy had attended the previous Saturday. The problem wasn't the course or the weather or the other players in attendance; it was Nick.

At work a day earlier, the CEO of his company had made a comment in a meeting that seemed dismissive of Nick and his leadership ability. Nick was angry, annoyed, hurt, worried – all at once. He hadn't yet mastered "What's the Intent?" and "Ask Clarifying Questions", so he reacted in an Ordinary way: stewing about the comment, replaying it in his mind, wondering what his CEO had really meant, speculating why he had spoken so harshly, wondering if others in the meeting also doubted his leadership. He slept poorly that night, and he continued to stew the next day during the tournament. He was riddled with fear of losing his job, and he was also angry at himself for reacting passively. Why hadn't he responded with this sharp comment, or that one, or a third?

Nick hadn't seen Tommy in a while and had been eager to catch up, but he couldn't pay attention to what his friend was saying. Nick was so upset and unable to concentrate that he wound up leaving the tournament early.

Sensing that Nick's emotions were still running high, I prompted him to consider the senior leader's likely intent. After a few minutes of conversation, he concluded that his CEO probably hadn't meant his comment the way he had received it. "Interesting," I said. "So let's think about this. Because you didn't use the tools, you just spent an entire day obsessing needlessly."

"I sure did," he said.

"As a result, you squandered the precious time that you were going to spend with Tommy."

"Uh-huh."

"And you'd been planning this day for how long?"

"Six months."

"So how do you feel?"

He sighed. "Terrible. I hate that I put myself through this. I hate that I wasted Tommy's time. I'm ashamed of myself, actually."

"Well, good news," I said, "You're going to get a redo. You wasted a day, so now you owe yourself one. You're going to call Tommy and find another day within the next month that you can spend together. This is going to be a weekday, and you're going to take it off entirely from work. You're not going to do anything work related. Nothing. No phone calls. No emails. You're not even going to *think* about work. You're just going to have fun and be present with your friend, as you intended."

Nick was nervous about taking an entire day off. He couldn't remember the last time he'd done that. He managed a sales team of fifteen, and they were busy making an aggressive, extended push for new clients that hopefully would allow them to ramp up their numbers later in the year. He worried that if he wasn't around to make decisions and offer guidance, someone could make a mistake and lose a potential account.

I reminded Nick that his tendency toward micromanaging others was something that he needed to work on, so forcing himself to take a day off would further his growth. His team members, whom he'd hand selected and who were all strong performers, would be just fine. Indeed, as they noticed his efforts to find balance in his life, they might follow his lead and try to do the same. Nick needed to be willing to trust them to get the job done without constantly looking over their shoulders.

It took Nick a week to wrap his mind around what I was suggesting – his fear of letting go ran so strong. But he eventually made some new plans with Tommy. The two of them played hooky on a Thursday, going bowling, seeing a movie, having a great dinner – just like old times.

When Nick returned to work the next day, he felt energized, much more than he'd expected. His emotions had got the better of him during the golf tournament, but now that he'd given himself back the joy that he'd lost, he felt a new sense of control. He was even more motivated than before to use "What's the Intent?" and his other tools to manage himself better. Since his team members had worked productively in his absence, he also had proven to himself that he could ease up and not be so vigilant. Going forward, he'd feel comfortable trusting his team more. He realized that his job wasn't in jeopardy and that his sensitivity to his CEO's remark had diminished his and his team's productivity.

Tracking Your Time

I share this episode to illustrate a foundational tool I use with clients called "Credits and Debits". You can think of this as a meta-technique of sorts, one that you can deploy using an old-fashioned notebook, a spreadsheet on your computer, or a note-taking app on your phone. It's a way of tracking the progress you're making and spurring yourself to do even more work on yourself in the future.

Let's say you use "What's the Intent?" or one of the other strategies I'll teach you in this book and that as a result you turn what would have been a forty-five-minute conversation with a team member into fifteen minutes. Congratulations: you just saved yourself thirty minutes. You can log that into your notebook as a credit. By the same token, if you spent a good two hours swirling, replaying an apparent insult because you *didn't* use one of the tools I'll show you, you log that time as a debit.

Most days, your debits and credits will likely be small – a few minutes up to a couple of hours. If that's the case, you can consider them cumulatively at the end of each week. Do the maths, and if you're running a negative balance, you owe yourself that time. You'll have to make it up by using the tools more intensely and regularly to save time the following week. If you're running a positive balance, you've got yourself a bit of leeway for times when you falter, and you can also put that extra time toward priorities in your life: exercising more, spending more time with your family, completing a special project at work or at home, and so on. If, as in Nick's case, you find yourself wasting a larger chunk of time, you can consider that a special debit and make plans to give yourself back that time. In this way, week in and week out, a concern with time can motivate your growth efforts and help you track your progress.

"Credits and Debits" is a fun, energetic approach to personal awareness and growth that you can deploy in tandem with the other tools. Remember when you were a kid and you earned small amounts of cash that you diligently put into the bank? You got a statement at the end of the month that told you how much you had saved and spent. I, at least, always found it satisfying to peruse that bank statement to see how I was doing. You can create a similar credit and debit sheet to track your progress toward developing an Exceptional mindset. This makes sense, since in our professional lives, time really is our most important currency.

Date	Debit (min)	Credit (min)	Event
10/4	15	-	Distracted by sales meeting
12/4	-	10	Ended unproductive discussion
13/4	-	12	Used my tool to save time
15/4	18	-	Swirled out based on comment Jane made to me about my team
18/4	-	12	Prepared team for IT discussion using my tool for efficiency
20/4	67	-	Swirled about Jack calling me out in a meeting; then conversed with Bill, Jane and Sam
21/4	-	120	Took two hours off to pay back some debits

Sample "Credits and Debits" logbook

I've found that tracking the time we save thanks to the tools or lose by not using them has a number of benefits. First, by holding ourselves accountable, we become more aware of the time we're frittering away thanks to our habitual ways of reacting. When our fears lead us to swirl about something that's ridiculous, nonproductive or immature and we know we must debit ourselves, we gain a tremendous awareness of "Oh, shit, I just burned fifteen minutes on this nonsense." We discover that our Ordinary ways of operating are costing us, sucking up our time and preventing us from achieving our goals. We learn that there *is* an opportunity to clear out a 25th hour – that the fifteen minutes we lose here and there because we're upset or engaged in a meaningless conversation really add up!

On the flip side, tracking our time energizes us to keep working on ourselves. When we save time using a tool, it feels great, even more so when we decide to put that time toward something that gives us joy and satisfaction. When you get to play tennis in the afternoon, visit a museum or take your kid out for ice cream because you saved a couple of hours on a meeting you managed Exceptionally, it's sensational – you feel as though you just won a prize! One of my clients who loves doing home improvement projects used his newfound time to stroll at his leisure up and down the aisles of a hardware store. He was downright giddy. Many of us are hard drivers, and we struggle to let ourselves relax and achieve a sense of balance. If we know we've earned fifteen minutes or half an hour of time, we can feel that we have permission to take that extra time at the gym or check in on the phone with a loved one. We walk away with a more enriched and balanced life.

"Credits and Debits" also helps us to see past incorrect and self-limiting assumptions we might have about how we ought to operate. When we use a tool to shave thirty minutes off a meeting, we showcase to ourselves that we *can* operate more efficiently, and we feel motivated to make it a regular practice. Ditto for when we force ourselves to give back a chunk of time we squandered thanks to our emotional response. Nick didn't think he could afford to take an entire day away from his team without falling behind on everything, but in fact he could. Holding himself accountable with debits and credits prompted him to look inward and realize that *he* was the one who was thwarting himself. As it turned out, one of his team members later mentioned how productive he had been the day Nick was out since he'd had fewer meetings and could spend more time with clients. Hearing that, Nick felt inspired to lead his team in a whole new way, spending more time performing meaningful activities and less time micromanaging.

In using "Credits and Debits", it's important to distinguish between our responses that are rational and hence legitimate and those that arise on account of our emotions. Chrissy is a very smart, high-performing young analyst at a company I advise, but we almost didn't hire her. She couldn't seem to decide whether she wanted to come on board with us, even though our company was an amazing fit for her, she was unhappy in her current role and she had no other job offers on the table. "Well, you know," she told our HR recruiter, "the company is perfect, the role is perfect, everyone I've met is so nice. I just love the opportunity! But the commute would be a little tough, and I'm feeling a little unsettled, so I'm just not sure." Four days passed with no decision on Chrissy's part. Finally, our recruiter told her that we couldn't wait any longer and were pulling our offer. "Wait," she said. "I'll accept the job."

I'm thrilled that Chrissy decided to join us, but to my way of thinking, she owed herself four days because of her indecision. You might think that I'm wrong: shouldn't we take our time and ponder the pros and cons when making an important decision like this? Yes, in many cases, that might be appropriate. If Chrissy had been considering three competing offers, she might well have wanted to take the time to analyse the pros and cons and to see what her kitchen cabinet thought. She also might have wanted to do so had she had an offer only from us but was ambivalent about it.

As it happened, she had known from the beginning that she wanted to join our company, but her deep-seated fears and anxieties had prevented her from pulling the trigger. She'd delayed because she hadn't been managing herself well. She'd spent those days talking through the decision with people in her life, hoping they'd be able to talk her out of her fears so that she could accept the job that she already knew she wanted. She'd spent hours listing the pros and cons for herself, again trying to outwit her fears. We've all done this at some point, haven't we?

Swirling over a decision you've already made and seeking reinforcement and validation from others *isn't* legitimate. It's Ordinary, plain and simple. If Chrissy had used a tool I'll discuss later called "What's the Worst Thing That Can Happen?", she'd have been able to surface her fears and calm herself in five minutes or less. If she'd been afraid of not liking her new job, this tool would have led her to remind herself that she was young, smart and ambitious and that she had a great résumé. In a worst-case scenario, she could leave after six months and get a new job. No big deal! The path to a decision would have been clear.

I stand by my contention that Chrissy owes herself four days. As for you, it's so important in specific situations to think about how you're responding to challenging events. How much of your behaviour was useful, healthy and productive? And how much of it was simply you allowing your emotions to get the better of you? Be honest! And then use "Credits and Debits" to log in the time you wasted.

Perhaps the best thing about "Credits and Debits" is that it provides a way to accept accountability without becoming beholden to a boss, colleague, roommate, or anyone else. The tool encourages you to manage *yourself*, helping you structure your use of my other tools, which, by the way, are all also designed to help with self-management. Because you're in charge, you get to customize "Credits and Debits" to your own situation. As an example, most of my clients don't keep a logbook for very long; they might do it for a few months to get them into the habit of paying attention to the time they're saving and wasting. Once the habit becomes ingrained, they switch over to logging in credits and debits more informally. Rather than keeping a journal, they register throughout the day that they owe themselves or have gained a certain amount of time. They make sure either to use their tools more aggressively the next day or to allow themselves that extra fifteen minutes of relaxing over their morning coffee. Their internalization of the tool helps instill an enduring sense of balance that keeps them on track, working with the tools and racking up that 25th hour.

No More Long, Boring Meetings

Now that you know about "Credits and Debits", I'd like to help you jump-start the credit side of the ledger. Do you know how when you open a savings account or a new credit card, the company will often, as an incentive, give you a bit of cash or an initial stash of loyalty points to get you started? I'm going to do something similar – with a twist. I won't actually give you time on the credit side. Instead, I'll share with you a couple of strategies that will enable you to rack up credits much more quickly than you think. In fact, you'll be taking steps toward your 25th hour in just the next day or so. These strategies are geared to the workplace, but you can adapt them to social encounters in your personal life, too.

If you've had any experience in organizations, you know that one of the greatest time sucks is meetings. They're insidious! In surveys of managers, sizeable majorities report believing that meetings were excessive and hurting their productivity.[1] One report found that a company of a hundred people could save $2.5 million annually by slashing useless meetings, while a company of five thousand could save more than $100 million each year.[2] Most of us feel harried at work and unable to focus, beset by incoming information, including that which we encounter at meetings.[3] Experts have advanced any number of solutions, such as allowing for more open discussion, keeping meetings from running over their allotted time, and setting out clear goals for a meeting.

Although such measures can help, I have a simpler and extremely effective suggestion for you. I call it the "10 Per Cent Meeting Rule". When you're the one organizing or facilitating a meeting, challenge yourself to end it 10 per cent early. If you schedule a meeting for an hour, end it after fifty-four minutes at the latest. If it's a half hour, call it by minute twenty-seven. That extra six or three minutes is yours to use as you please. It's fascinating how much you can accomplish with these little pockets of time. You can answer email or texts, plan dinner, have a quick conversation with someone or, how about this, just *think*.

When used along with "Credits and Debits", the "10 Per Cent Meeting Rule" isn't really a time management tool; it's a productivity tool. When I know I'm going to end a meeting early, I don't slack on what I need to cover, because that's not an option. Instead, I become more connected to the material at hand, and I try harder to run the conversation efficiently. I focus on getting in, covering what we need to cover, and getting out, with a minimum of time wasted. We've all been to meetings that drag, where people blather on just to hear themselves talk. When you're focused on ending 10 per cent early, that doesn't happen.

The enhanced productivity continues after the meeting, too. I don't know about you, but I'm scheduled every minute of the day. When I have a sixty-minute meeting that runs sixty minutes, I don't have time to hit the restroom, grab a snack, prepare for my next meeting or catch a breath. With six minutes of extra time or even just three, I can do all of these things. When I get to the next meeting, I'm calmer and more focused, so I'm able to pay attention and operate more effectively.

Depending on how many meetings you run, you might be able to get to your 25th hour right away using the "10 Per Cent Meeting Rule". If you deploy the rule in five one-hour meetings over the course of a day, you're already saved thirty minutes; you're halfway there. Repeat that day after day, and you're saving tons of time. With your 25th hour or even just a portion of it, you can do other things that give you joy. That in turn makes you more productive. To take but one example, I do some of my best thinking not when I'm at my desk but when I'm taking a walk, especially on the beach. I'm sure you also have leisure pursuits that not only fill your tank but give you space to think more creatively and have epiphanies. Ending meetings early gives you more opportunity for such fertile moments.

It's crazy to think that something as simple as ending a meeting 10 per cent early can impact your ability to get stuff done so dramatically, but it absolutely can. And there are still other benefits. If you're a leader and you end a meeting early, you've instantly gained a ton of credibility. Everyone around you will appreciate a bit of extra time, and they'll appreciate that the time they do spend with you is highly productive. They'll start talking about how much they love attending your meetings. Soon you'll become the preferred partner, leader or colleague, known as someone who can run a meeting for maximum impact. You'll inspire others to start ending their meetings early, too. All because you challenged yourself to run the meeting more efficiently.

You might wonder whether you can end meetings early while still accomplishing what you need to. To help with that, here's another tool: the "Quick Check-in". How many times have you sat in a one-hour meeting only to spend the first ten minutes on meaningless chitchat? Someone will say, "How's your weekend?" or "I heard you went to the party last night," and a conversation will ensue that interests maybe three of the eight people there. Conversations like this are common – there's probably one happening right now. The three people who are interested might get something out of the conversation, but for the other five people, that's ten minutes of their life they can't get back. And nobody in the room is doing any actual work. If eight people are present, that translates into eighty minutes of lost productivity. Multiply that by the number of meetings that occur in your organization, and you can see just how devastatingly wasteful they are.

You might object that friendly chitchat is important because it allows participants to build rapport and feel more connected. Won't meetings start to seem impersonal if we force ourselves to get down to business? That's where the "Quick Check-in" can help. Instead of all that mindless chatter, I start my meetings by going around the table and asking everyone present, myself included, to say one word (and only one) that best captures their current state of mind. I ask them to be truthful and show real vulnerability if necessary. People might say "busy", "distracted", "caffeinated" or "rested". If you've had the flu and are still dragging, you might say "recovering". If your daughter just graduated from college the previous weekend, you might say "elated".

With up to ten people, it takes less than a minute to perform this exercise. In that single minute, everyone mentally checks into the conversation. Everyone has a sense of how their colleagues are doing and what state of mind they're in. If someone utters a word that is intriguing to you, you can go up to that person after the meeting to inquire about it. "Hey," you might say, "you said 'recovering'. What were you recovering from? Is anything going on?" You're still having a more involved, rapport-building conversation, but you're not taking up the group's time to do it. If there are colleagues in the meeting with whom you're friendly, you can still chat with them, but after the meeting is over and using the extra six minutes (in a one-hour meeting) that the group has saved by ending early.

You can probably find other ways to save 10 per cent of your meeting time, but in many cases "Quick Check-in" alone will do the trick. You might even save more than 10 per cent. One regular meeting I run is scheduled for thirty minutes. Depending on what's happening and what we need to discuss, we're sometimes done in as little as nine. That's one minute of checking in and eight of substantive business. I announce to the team that I'm giving them back twenty-one minutes, or 70 per cent of the allocated time. Am I going to log that in as a credit on my own "Credits and Debits" worksheet? Absolutely!

On some days, I might use some of that extra twenty-one minutes to pull members of the team aside and discuss other business. Or I might decide to end the meeting and then hold a portion of the team back to discuss another topic for a few minutes, so we don't have to schedule a separate meeting. Or I might keep the full team assembled because one of them has something they want us all to discuss together. But much of the time, everyone just gets nearly a half hour of valuable time tacked back onto their day, to use as they please.

If you're not the meeting's leader but simply a participant, I encourage you to share "Quick Check-in" with the person running the show. Clarify that you're not trying to criticize or interfere with how they run meetings but rather alert them to a tool that has been proven to boost productivity. The vast majority of my clients who have spread the word about "Quick Check-in" report receiving a positive reception from those in charge. Far from causing offence, their Exceptional behaviour wins them bonus points.

The 50 Per Cent Phone Call Rule

I've discussed the productivity benefits of "Credits and Debits" and the other two time-related tools, but let's remember their more basic purpose: to help advance our personal growth and development. All of the tools I'll introduce in this book will save you time, and that's fantastic. But the *way* they get you to that time savings is by prompting or helping you manage yourself better – helping you become more aware of your fears and other negative emotions, managing them so that they don't overwhelm your life and prevent you from reaching your goals. Time management – carving out that 25th hour – is the pathway toward the deeper change we ultimately want and need. By helping you track that time saving as well as the time you're currently wasting by failing to manage yourself well, "Credits and Debits" gives you a structure for becoming a better, calmer, more effective person.

If my clients' experience is any indication, the progress you'll see when using "Credits and Debits" alongside my other tools will be significant, even transformational. One client of mine, Bobby, took the "10 Per Cent Meeting Rule" and ran with it. Forget about meetings, and forget about 10 per cent: he challenged himself to cut the time he spent on every phone call he took at work by 50 per cent. A call with a team member that used to take him thirty minutes he'd handle in just fifteen. Did he reach that goal every time? No. But by approaching every phone call with an eye toward time savings, he profoundly changed his outlook on his work and his relationship with his team.

Like Nick from the beginning of this chapter, Bobby struggled with micromanaging. Resolving to slash his phone call time in half not only forced him to handle calls more efficiently; it meant that he simply couldn't stay abreast of every small issue his team was dealing with. Like it or not, he'd have to overcome his fears, trust team members more, and give them the leeway they needed to perform their best. He'd be there to advise on big questions they might have, but otherwise, he'd stay out of the way. Along with some urging by me, his "50 Per Cent Phone Call Rule" gave him the motivation and structure he needed to finally lean into his fears and stop hovering over his team's every move. As he recalibrated as a manager, team members responded by taking much more ownership over their work and exceeding his expectations. It was a massive shift for Bobby, a big step on his way toward managing himself and becoming Exceptional. And it all started with a seemingly insignificant shift in how he handled phone calls.

Think about the small adjustments you might be able to make to rack up a positive balance on "Credits and Debits". Start by keeping an actual notebook, and then, as you feel ready, give yourself permission to wean yourself off it. Make this tool and the others discussed here your own. If you find that interactions with a particular person are wasting your time, challenge yourself to cut them by 20 per cent. Or challenge your entire team as a group to cut meeting times or phone calls by 10 per cent. This is *your* tool. It's about you managing you. What can you do right now to get yourself that 25th hour?

Find Your 25th Hour: Credits and Debits

In a notebook or on a piece of paper, create a simple T chart, with a Debits column on the left and Credits column on the right. Leave room on the far left for a description. Keep a log for one week of the moments when you used your tools in an Exceptional way and record how much time you saved as credits. Similarly, record as debits the time you lost when you exhibited Ordinary behaviour. Start a new sheet each week and pay attention to how many consecutive positive weeks you rack up.

Part II

How to Stay Focused and Productive in the Face of Daily Adversity

As you practise using the basic strategies and exercises from part I, you'll start to become more aware of your habitual reactions in the moment and learn to control them so that you can better pursue your goals. Yet it's easy to veer off track. Despite our best intentions, the small, perceived setbacks we experience every day in social situations can claim our attention, causing us to lapse into inefficient, emotion-based behaviour patterns. To manage ourselves better and develop an Exceptional mindset, and to get that wonderful 25th hour, we must become expert at handling daily adversity, stopping these troublesome moments from spiralling out of control and dragging us down. Here's a series of techniques, strategies and concepts that you can use individually and in combination with one another to stay focused and productive when life doesn't quite go as you'd hoped.

Four

The Simple Act of Slowing Down

Now that we're a few chapters into this book, I'd like you to try something. Think of a place that you find completely calming and relaxing – your happy place. It might be the tree-lined street where you go jogging a few times a week. Or the café you love to visit on Sunday mornings. Or the picturesque creek where you used to swim during your childhood summers. Or the spectacular beach you visit each summer. You get the idea. Just forget all about this book, your work and your other responsibilities and imagine this place. Spend maybe four or five seconds, lingering longer if you wish. Reflect on a few details of this place that make it special for you – maybe the sun filtering through the trees, the great coffee smell in that café, the feeling of the cold water in the creek when you jumped in, the sound of the surf at the beach.

How do you feel? More relaxed? Calmer? You just performed "Focal Point", a tool that's enormously helpful in the face of daily adversity. Quite often in life, something happens that throws us off balance. We receive bad news, a colleague utters a disparaging comment, our child talks back to us, our spouse forgets to do the dishes. It's Ordinary in such situations to react, allowing our emotions to dictate our actions, often in ways that hurt us and cost us time.

Scientists refer to this quick gut response as "amygdala hijacking". The amygdala is an evolutionarily primitive part of our brains associated with our emotional functioning, including our fear response. When we're under stress and experience a perceived threat, our amygdala activates, bypassing parts of the brain responsible for a more reasoned, thoughtful response, and leading us to behave impulsively. Only later, as other parts of the brain come back online, do we start to ponder what an appropriate, rational response might have been. By that time, it's too late; we've acted in ways that will probably embroil us in drama and internal spiralling, costing us needless time.[1]

"Focal Point" lets us stop the hijacking of our brain so that we can regain composure and respond more intentionally. Instead of rushing into an instinctive reaction that will probably be informed by that sneaky old Devil on our shoulder, we can choose to take a beat first, bringing ourselves back ever so briefly to our happy place. That tiny moment of calm and well-being recentres us, opening up a space outside our emotions. As we regain focus, we can call up one of our tools to form a more considered, Exceptional response, saving the time we would have wasted had we responded in an Ordinary way. Quite likely, we'll also save ourselves the trouble of having to apologize for our defensive, Ordinary behaviour.

I first began practising and teaching "Focal Point" years ago while working with Mark, the young entrepreneur I mentioned in the introduction who was struggling with his startup. As I got to know him, I found that he was excessively amped up all the time. He had one speed: *screamingly fast*. In his mind, he was always thinking, *Go go go go go go go*, never taking a moment to slow down. Because he was rushing, he made mistakes, which fed his fears and insecurities about his leadership ability. His frantic pace also gave the Devil on his shoulder free rein during moments of adversity, leaving him spinning with thoughts about his lack of ability or the inevitable failure of his startup. All too often, he wound up making poor, fear-based decisions.

Somehow, I had to get Mark to slow down so that he could shake free of his emotional response and do things differently. One day as I was sitting with him, an answer came to me. I thought back to an experience I'd had while attending Lamaze class with my wife. The instructor taught her how to mentally remove herself from the physical pain she would experience during childbirth by thinking of her happy place. While she was in labour, she kept photos of sunsets, sunrises, beaches or other relaxing spots in her line of sight. Looking at the photos, she could distance herself from the pain she felt. It was such a simple idea, but an effective one. As research has shown, visualizations can have a profound effect on us, not only managing pain but soothing anxiety, enabling us to focus better, and even helping our immune system.[2]

It dawned on me that what works for women in labour might also help a hyped-up twentysomething entrepreneur who was struggling to manage himself. Telling Mark about what I'd learned in Lamaze class, I asked him what his happy place was. He described a cabin in the woods that his family had visited during his childhood. As he talked about that place, he smiled and his eyes lit up; clearly it was deeply meaningful and calming for him. He began making a practice of pausing and visualizing the cabin, which enabled him to calm down a bit so that he could remember to use his other tools. Instead of losing himself in a difficult moment, he pushed back at the Devil on his shoulder and gave his Angel a chance to express itself.

"Focal Point" isn't just a tool to help you stay focused in the workplace; you can use it to handle difficult situations in every part of your life. During arguments with your spouse, don't just respond defensively or escalate the tension; visualize your happy place, and then mobilize one of the tools. During tense encounters with your kids, go to your focal point to catch yourself before you lash out. Then mobilize a tool to allow for a more productive conversation. I use "Focal Point" all the time when something triggers me. As a client of mine put it, "It's literally two seconds of 'Take a breath, put your best foot forward. How do you want to show up?'"

Those two seconds can make all the difference. The CEO of a firm I advise was meeting with investors to ask for more capital. One of them began asking tough questions that put the CEO on the defensive. Rather than pushing back against the investor's questions, telling the investor that they were wrong and offering proof, the CEO went to his happy place, the cockpit of an aeroplane he owns and pilots. That calmed him enough so that he could ask himself about the investor's intent in seeming to show so much scepticism. He realized that it had nothing to do with him and that it instead reflected pressure that the investor was feeling from his own boss. The CEO responded by asking a clarifying question. A conversation that might have spiralled out of control, damaging the relationship, took a more positive turn. The CEO saved hours he might have spent afterward struggling with the Ucks and commiserating with his team about that annoying investor.

Some of my clients find "Focal Point" indispensable as a way of dealing with their anxiety and anticipation about what *might* happen. Samantha is a wickedly smart senior leader who suffers from a stubborn, deeply ingrained perfectionistic streak. She danced competitively as a child, and her strict, excessively rigid teacher got her into the habit of noticing and correcting even the smallest imperfections in her performances. Transferring that rigid, uncompromising attitude into the workplace, Samantha finds that her perfectionism causes all kinds of problems. She reacts defensively upon receiving feedback. She stresses out about tiny perceived deficiencies in her performance that aren't really problems, wasting time and effort spiralling while trying to correct them. And she feels a great deal of anxiety, worrying that her performance in a presentation or meeting isn't perfect and that others will perceive her as a failure.

As I pointed out to her, such anxiety was unwarranted. In advance of a big speech she had to give, for instance, she had no data suggesting that she would fail to deliver. But such rational arguments on my part didn't help her. She had convinced herself that she was going to fail, and she was terrified. What did help her was "Focal Point". When she felt overwhelmed by anxiety because she was about to give a speech, she brought herself back to her happy place. That calmed her and gave her an opportunity to use a tool called "I'm Really Good at What I Do" to neutralize her anxiety and remind herself of her competence.

When we pull ourselves out of an amygdala hijacking situation, life becomes easier in ways that might surprise us. One of my clients talks fondly about his happy place, the peaceful farm where he grew up. Closing his eyes, he imagines himself sitting on the porch of his family's farmhouse, smelling scents wafting over from a nearby alfalfa field. After, say, ten or twelve seconds of this, he sometimes gets flashes of insight. It might occur to him how to handle a difficult business problem that has been befuddling him all weekend. He had been pondering and worrying about the issue for thirty or forty hours, but with just twelve seconds of visualization, the solution has become clear.

Think of the times in your day when someone stresses you out and triggers negative emotions, whether it's fear, anxiety, anger, disappointment, embarrassment or more. Reflect on how your body feels at these moments. Maybe your pulse quickens, your throat goes dry, your mind wanders and spins, your palms get sweaty, your face flushes, you develop a pit in your stomach. You now have a strategy for staving off these physiological responses. Instead of freaking or lashing out and wasting time in the process, you can behave in more thoughtful, mature ways that reflect your values and goals. You also can create opportunities for creative insights that otherwise might have been impossible.

Pressing the Pause Button

Probing deeper, we find that the magic of "Focal Point" doesn't come just from the act of visualizing but from something else: the decision to slow down. When you take a few seconds to go to your happy place, you're pausing the situation you're in midstream so that you can get your bearings. I consider that the very essence of self-management. In fact, whether you visualize your happy place or not, making a habit of pausing in the course of a social situation can benefit you. It's so helpful and fundamental that I consider it a tool in its own right, what I call "Pause Button".

Is a colleague saying something that pisses you off? Don't open your mouth. Just don't! Press the pause button. Create a long, uncomfortable moment of silence – five to ten seconds or more. Maybe throw in a little head nod or something, so that the other person knows you're still with them. You might not be getting the full physiological benefits that come with actively visualizing a happy place and calming your body, but you're still giving yourself a moment to get past the flood of emotions so that you can reassert control.

But you're doing much more than that. Have you ever been in a conversation with someone who interrupts the rhythm with a long pause? It's unexpected, surprising, maybe even puzzling. *What is this person doing?* you wonder. *Did they hear my question? Are they going to answer me? Are they meditating? What the hell's going on?*

That person has just thrown you off balance, giving themselves some power over you. By breaking up the rhythm of the conversation, they've focused your attention on them, and they've put the onus on *you* to figure out what to say next. Conversely, if you're the one pausing, you're taking charge of the situation and giving yourself valuable time to think about it, understand the other person's intent, and quickly develop a strategy for handling it. You can reflect on your objective and what you might say or do to achieve it. And you can think about the likely impact of what you might want to say on others.

Many of us ramble when we're nervous or fearful, trying to fill empty space so that we can avoid awkward silence. Please fight that urge! Pausing allows you to exercise more control, because you're in better control of *yourself*. By contrast, when you react emotionally or when you blather on because you're wigged out by empty silence, people sense it. They understand that *they're* in control – or rather, that you've ceded them control over you.

Imagine you're sitting across from your boss, who just told you that you're being terminated. If you're like many people, you might express surprise, ask why you're being fired, or answer questions your boss has of you. But what if, upon hearing the news, you just pause and say nothing? What if you let that pause linger and then simply say, "Understood" before getting up and leaving. Can you imagine the impact that might have? Yes, you've been terminated, but you just turned the tables, undermining your boss's power. Now your boss is wondering – maybe even worrying about – what *you're* thinking. Sometimes not saying something, or saying very little, is the most powerful response of all.

Pausing also helps because it creates space for *others* to come up with solutions. One person I coach, a doctor of physical therapy named Maggie, often uses "Pause Button" in her encounters with patients. As she's working on their physical ailments, they open up to her, describing problems they're having in their lives. Rather than immediately interjecting her own opinions, which might reflect her emotions or habitual ways of thinking, she'll pause and listen, contenting herself with serving as a sounding board. When she does this, she finds that her patients tend to arrive at their own solutions, without her having to suggest anything. Since *they* came up with the solutions themselves, they feel stronger and more empowered than if she had told them the answer. Their epiphanies tend to transform them more, since they find it easier to internalize an idea they discovered for themselves.

As an alternative to “Focal Point”, Maggie has developed her own way of pausing that you might find helpful. She takes a breath, closes her eyes for a moment, and tries to cue into her body and how it feels. She asks herself, *What are we doing here? What's happening right now? Might I chime in with an idea, or am I better off just continuing to listen? If I feel an urge to offer an idea, is there some emotional need of mine that's behind that?* All of this happens within the space of a few seconds. Sometimes she does offer a suggestion of her own; other times, she just continues to listen. Pausing gives her the freedom to respond intentionally and follow her intuition.

“Focal Point” and “Pause Button” are so simple, yet so powerful. Think of the hours you'll save when you aren't reacting to every negative thought or situation that comes your way and when you give yourself the mental space to become self-aware in the moment and behave more deliberately. Try these tools out for yourself. And as in previous chapters, don't feel limited by my descriptions of these tools. Experiment with your own, unique way of pausing, and customize the questions you ask yourself. As I think you'll find, the time you spend *not speaking* during a social interaction might be some of the most fruitful moments of all.

Find Your 25th Hour: Pause Button

First, decide on your focal point – your happy place that automatically brings a smile to your face. Then, during your next three conversations with others, experiment with including an uncomfortable pause. Don't wait for the perfect moment – just do it! Fight any discomfort you have, and let the silence linger for at least ten seconds. If you wish, count out the seconds in your head as you visualize your focal point. How do others respond? Do you notice a change in the dynamic? How was the silence for you? Where did your mind go? How did you feel after the pause? Were you clearer and more focused? More able to respond rationally rather than emotionally? Now that you've tried it, integrate "Pause Button" into your daily routine. In moments of adversity, inject an even greater sense of calm by using "Focal Point".

Five

Make Everything Your Fault

When I was twenty-two and only a couple of weeks into my job at the radio sales and marketing company Interep, my boss called me into his office one day and asked me about the status of a report I was working on – would I have it ready the next week or not?

It was a simple yes-or-no question, but it left me feeling anxious and insecure. I hadn't finished the report, and it seemed that my boss was already expecting it on his desk. Trying to cover for myself, I responded by offering up an incoherent series of excuses, pointing to other tasks I had on my plate, problems with the input I was receiving from others, and so on. It was a long-winded, rambling and frankly ridiculous monologue that must have stretched on for two or three minutes. As I was speaking, I noticed my boss gazing at me in disbelief, grinning faintly. When I finished, he paused for a moment and said, "Wow, you're a defensive one. I just asked you a yes-or-no question! I didn't expect that you'd have completed the report by now."

If I'd replied simply and honestly, telling my boss that the report wasn't complete but that I'd have it to him by the end of the week as scheduled, the moment would have passed and everything would have been fine. In asking the question, his intent wasn't to pressure me but rather to see whether I needed any help or support. Instead, I'd highlighted my insecurity and lack of self-confidence. Thankfully, he didn't hold it against me. On the contrary, he was so amused by it that he started calling me "Defensive" as a nickname – and never stopped. We remain in touch to this day, and he still calls me that, decades later. "Hey, Defensive," he'll say, "where do you want to meet for lunch?"

I'm hardly alone in my impulse to deny or deflect when I feel criticized. All of us do it. A perceived attack or insult triggers our fight-or-flight response, and then *boom!* the Devil on our shoulder takes over. We see this all the time in corporate contexts. The CEO of a company comes in and asks a subordinate to explain subpar results. The subordinate protests that it wasn't their fault – the sales managers were to blame, or operations, or even the CEO themself for setting unrealistic goals. Companies waste untold amounts of time in arguments about whose fault it was and misguided attempts at change that fail to address the *real* issues hampering progress. This is completely Ordinary behaviour.

Many of us might not even realize that we're seeking to avoid blame; that's how locked in our habit is. We're socialized from a young age to respond in kind when we perceive that someone is attacking us; we equate that with being strong, forceful and powerful. When we get hit, we're told that we're supposed to hit back harder. Some of us also might be inclined toward defensiveness on account of our personalities or childhood experiences that left us with low self-esteem.[1]

Defensive responses are so prevalent that psychologists as far back as Sigmund Freud have talked about such behaviour and come up with complicated models defining it.[2] They've also noted how corrosive defensive reactions are to relationships. In fact, the respected psychologist John Gottman regards it as one of the four communication patterns that can foreshadow a relationship's demise.[3]

Earlier in my career, I hated being called defensive and tried my best to work on that behaviour. As the years passed, I noticed that many others, including my own clients, were wasting time and harming their relationships by attempting to deny and deflect. Sometimes the criticisms they were fielding were correct, and they couldn't hear them, take responsibility and make needed adjustments. Other times when their colleagues, bosses or partners were wrongly taking them to task, their defensive habits prompted them to respond in ways that were needlessly harsh, off-putting and antagonistic. This in turn sparked a defensive reaction in others, creating drama and virtually guaranteeing that they'd waste time stewing or fighting.

Somehow, I thought, I need to help people – including myself – overcome powerful, ego-based responses. I need to help them reprogramme their thinking, neutralizing that voice in their heads telling them to put up barriers and lash back when attacked.

What I came up with was a tool called "It's My Fault". It was inspired by an experience I'd had back in elementary school. We were on the playground at recess, and a teacher's aide, spotting a candy wrapper on the ground, asked me very nicely if I'd mind picking it up. I resisted at first, instinctively defending myself. "It's not mine. I didn't drop it," I said. The aide agreed that it wasn't mine but reminded me that she was simply asking me to do her a favour.

Now, many years later, I wondered: What will happen if I ask people – again, including myself – to run through a mental exercise in which they lightheartedly take responsibility for *everything*, even problems or misfortunes that they obviously didn't create? Instead of hearing that voice of defensiveness all the time, implicitly absolving us of responsibility, what if we were to go to the opposite extreme, poking fun at the very idea of blame? That word as well as others such as "fault" and "mistake" carry such negative connotations for most of us that they almost always elicit a defensive or Ordinary response. It's about time that we neutralized these words with a little humour, don't you think?

Right now, away from any kind of conflict situation, pause for a moment. If there was traffic during your commute, tell yourself that it was your fault. Did your neighbor's garbage can fall over, making a mess? Your fault. Was your flight late? Yep, that's your fault, too. Did the server at the restaurant mess up your lunch order? *Totally* your fault. Did a sudden snowstorm cause the authorities in your town to cancel school for the day? Again, that's completely on you.

Now, you obviously bear no responsibility for any of these mishaps. And that's the point. By having you take responsibility for *everything*, to the point of ridiculousness, the tool removes the tremendous emotional baggage that the word "fault" normally carries. When we run through this exercise a few times, we start to realize that it's okay: we can take responsibility for miscues or failures that really *are* our fault. We don't need to get so defensive about it.

"It's My Fault" isn't just something to practise on the sidelines; you can also use it in a moment when you're under attack. The next time your boss, colleague or professor confronts you about a disappointing result, mentally run through "It's My Fault" rather than reacting defensively. Doing so might open space for you to help solve the problem. You'll start to ask yourself whether some portion of the responsibility really *does* reside with you, and that realization can lead you to intercede directly with others and help to drive toward a solution. You'll have saved stretches of time that you would have spent on the idle exercise of blaming others, even as the problem festered. And you'll leave others around you feeling respected and heard while also building trust.

This exercise is one of my favourites because it's wacky; most of my clients don't understand where I'm going with it until they try it themselves and make it their own. But then, after some practice, it works for them every time, defusing situations in their minds so that they can make better choices. Whether or not they actually bear blame, telling themselves that it's their fault reminds them not to deny or deflect but instead to respond in a more neutral and Exceptional way. This prevents them from triggering defensive responses in others, allowing them to avoid unhealthy and unproductive spirals of conflict.

Transforming Relationships – and Our Careers

To understand the power of "It's My Fault", consider a situation involving my client Ellie, whom we met briefly in chapter 2. As the CFO at her company, Ellie found herself at loggerheads with her colleague Nikki, who served as head of Human Resources. Both were high-achieving women who successfully balanced their careers with their roles as mums. Each respected the other outside work. But in meetings, the two would go at it over the smallest of issues, often in passive-aggressive ways. Such exchanges wasted everyone else's time, diluted their authority in the eyes of their team members, and left them bickering and stewing long afterward.

Looking back on it, Ellie suspects that she'd built up some jealousy toward Nikki. While as CFO Ellie often found herself in the position of being a Debbie Downer in the organization, reminding other leaders of budget constraints, Nikki didn't have that constraint. Others saw her as "the company therapist", Ellie says, someone who could "do no wrong".

Realizing how much damage her jealousy-fuelled behaviour was doing to their relationship and in turn to their teams and the company, Ellie decided that she had to take steps to rein it in. She used several tools I discuss in this book, but it was "It's My Fault" that led to a breakthrough.

One day after a meeting, Nikki texted Ellie to express her frustration at something Ellie had said. Ellie was tempted to reply with a denial or an accusation of her own, as she often had in the past, which would only have kept the wheels of conflict turning. Instead, she did something radically different. She told herself that yes, it was her fault. And so was the bad economy. And the shortage of filters for the coffee machine in the break room. And the mistake another colleague had made on his presentation. Now, of course, she didn't believe any of that. It was just her reminder to lighten up and not take accusations of fault, whether from Nikki or anyone else, so seriously.

Having short-circuited her impulse to react defensively, Ellie could look at what had happened between her and Nikki more rationally and craft a better, more reasonable response. Actually, she thought, maybe she *had* come across as too antagonistic or harsh with Nikki, even if she hadn't necessarily intended her words to come out that way. She conveyed that sentiment to Nikki. As she recalled, "I was like, 'You know what? You're right. I could have explained my thinking more clearly and gently, so I was wrong. I appreciate the feedback. I apologize, and I will take a different approach next time.'"

Ellie's response made a huge impression on Nikki, who hadn't been expecting it. "Wow," she said, "I really appreciate that." From then on, their relationship began to improve. By shifting her own behaviour, Ellie guided Nikki to adjust hers, changing the dynamic of their interactions. Of course, Ellie had to continue using "It's My Fault" during tense moments to prevent the old dynamic from returning. But as she did, she found increasingly less hostility aimed in her direction. Instead of adversaries, the two became allies.

As Ellie reflected, she and Nikki now have "one of the strongest relationships in the entire company". In fact, they use their relationship as an example to help others in the company collaborate better. "When we are teaching certain skill sets to the organization, we will get up there and say, 'Okay, for those of you that have been with us a long time, you see how Nikki and I used to interact versus how we are now.' We talk about how we've adjusted to each other's working styles to be more effective."

This turn in their relationship has left Ellie with a greater understanding of the strength and power that comes when senior leaders accept responsibility and avoid the blame game. So many leaders evade accountability, refusing to speak honestly about challenges facing their organizations because they fear looking bad in front of their people. It's much stronger, she suggests, to speak transparently, acknowledging your own faults and limitations. "True confidence is to say when you're wrong," she says; it's not creating a veneer of perfection.

This insight doesn't just apply to leaders. For any of us, accepting responsibility rather than giving in to a knee-jerk defensiveness puts us in a stronger position, arousing others' admiration and increasing our influence and authority.

Back when I was in my mid-twenties and working at Interep as a mid-level manager, the chairman and CEO, Ralph, asked me and another colleague, Nadine, to make a presentation to the rest of his leadership team about some strategic initiatives we were planning to implement. Ralph had already approved the initiatives; in fact, they had been his idea. It was a big deal for me, a chance to make my mark in front of some of the organization's most senior leaders. Anxious to excel, I overprepared, loading myself with data points and other information to make a compelling case. I made sure that everything I said conformed to what Ralph had asked me to do.

When it came time to fly to New York City for the big meeting, I was ready. The meeting began, and everyone paid close attention as Nadine and I presented. After perhaps ten minutes, as I was describing a particular strategic initiative, Ralph cut me off. "Yeah," he said, "I don't think . . . Nah, we're not going to do that."

I was flabbergasted – and humiliated. To everyone else in the room, it must have seemed as though I didn't know what I was talking about or hadn't prepared. My instinct in that moment was to react by making some kind of excuse for myself or noting that I'd only been following Ralph's instructions. But I didn't do that. Since I'd been working on not behaving so defensively, I decided to simply take the lump, remarking casually to Ralph, "Oh, sorry, that must be on me." I then continued with my presentation.

Glancing around, I saw that everyone was taken aback by my

response – in a good way. They'd been expecting me to try to cover for myself, make excuses or somehow wiggle my way out of the situation. That's the Ordinary response, because when we're under attack in a setting like this we typically fear some bad consequence – losing our job, our influence or our power – and want to prevent it. I had chosen to see accepting responsibility as no big deal, which in fact it wasn't. That allowed me to casually accept responsibility and move on. Because I'd responded in that Exceptional way, I came across as self-assured and mature beyond my years. Most employees in their mid-twenties don't seem to belong in a boardroom with the bigwigs. That day, I very much did.

I also saved myself quite a bit of time that I would have otherwise wasted. Let's say I'd allowed myself to feel defensive in that moment and tried to save face. Afterward, I'd have spent hours, even days, continuing to feel demoralized, upset and insecure about my position. Overcome by anxiety, I'd have felt compelled to approach the fifteen other senior leaders in the room individually to explain the situation and defend my honour, telling them something such as "I just want you to know that Ralph was actually the one who told me to say that." Maybe we'd have commiserated privately about how often Ralph changed his mind or, alternatively, how malicious he was – how easy it was for him to throw people under the bus. I might have felt better in the moment, but I'd have wasted hours having the same conversation fifteen times over, and I'd have wasted those leaders' time as well. None of that happened. Instead, I used those hours to get my work done. If I'd been tracking debits and credits back then, I would have hit the jackpot on my way to a 25th hour!

Solve the Problem, Don't Create New Ones

A colleague of mine recently asked me if it *ever* makes sense to deflect or deny blame. What if you're accused of a serious misdeed that might affect your reputation or career prospects, and you know beyond a doubt that you're innocent? Surely, then, it makes sense to circle the wagons and protect yourself. You'd be a fool not to, right?

Wrong.

Of course, if you're accused of an actual crime and are involved in a formal legal proceeding, that's one thing – professing your innocence to law enforcement and to the courts is a necessity. But otherwise, a defensive response always works against you, as it creates a tone that makes resolution of problems more difficult or even impossible.

A client of mine, a senior executive at a large healthcare company, was working on a big project that required an investment in the tens of millions of dollars. For whatever reason, his boss, the company's president, neglected to let the board know about the investment. The board members learned about it only when they realized at one of their meetings that the organization was running tens of millions of dollars over budget. Not good – someone looked dangerously incompetent. The president, who was at the meeting, blamed my client for the oversight, even though he was the one who had been neglectful or forgetful. It was a hugely Ordinary thing to do.

A board member approached my client and pointed out the gap between budgeted and actual expenditures, suggesting that he was at fault. How did my client respond? In the Ordinary way. He got defensive, protesting (albeit in a calm voice) that he'd done nothing wrong; he'd provided the information in writing to his boss, and therefore the communication gap was his boss's fault. He tried to protect his position by commiserating with the board member, asking him why he thought the president had been so neglectful, and presenting written evidence to back up his contention that he was right and his boss wrong. Afterward, my client spent weeks amassing additional evidence, scouring old emails and meeting notes, and printing them out. What a massive and distracting time suck. He also stormed into his boss's office and accused him of throwing him under the bus.

My client's boss continued his Ordinary behaviour. He hit back to cover his own butt, asserting that my client had been supposed to include the investment in his division's financial planning but hadn't done so. A holy war between the two broke out in the company, roiling and distracting the leadership team. The controversy blew up to such an extent that it put the board in the position of having to adjudicate it and fire one of the two leaders.

Consider what might have happened had my client used "It's My Fault" when approached by that board member. He knows it's not really his fault. He has emails up the wazoo to prove it. But because he no longer feels the same kind of heaviness at being under attack, he can respond to the board member by saying something such as "Huh. Interesting. You know what? Let me look into this issue and get back to you. I'm curious what happened in the board meeting. What was the conversation?"

He could then have gone back to his boss. Instead of ripping him a new one because he's so angry, he could have said, "Hey, board member so-and-so just came into my office and had this really interesting question about how our spending is over budget by tens of millions of dollars. Help me understand what's happening there and why the board doesn't know about the spending plan we reviewed." Such a response would have put the onus on his boss to explain the situation, perhaps creating an opening for him to admit in private that he'd made a mistake. The two could have collaborated to figure out a solution that would keep their relationship – and both of their jobs – intact.

People make mistakes. And sometimes they blame us to cover them up. They provoke us. They bully us. But how we deal with these situations matters. Even if we're 100 per cent in the right, denying and deflecting doesn't help. The defensive, even hostile tone we're projecting engenders more of the same from others. It might leave us feeling good in the moment, but we serve our interests better by solving the problem at hand, not creating new ones. That means getting past our knee-jerk, ego-based response and reacting more thoughtfully so that we can get others on board to help us, even our accusers.

This point holds not just in the workplace but throughout our lives. In the grocery store when someone bumps their cart against ours, we can say, "Oh, I'm sorry" and move on with our shopping. Or we can say, "Get out of the way, you asshole," getting into an altercation that will leave us stewing and perhaps nursing a black eye. At home when our dog runs off and our spouse accuses us of forgetting to close the backyard gate, we could say, "Yep, that's my bad" and spend three short minutes going to the next-door neighbour's yard to bring Rover back. Or we could say, "I'm not getting him. You left the gate open last night, so why don't *you* get him," sparking an argument that will take forty-five minutes to unwind.

Who is at fault in these situations doesn't matter. It truly is irrelevant. If we behave in an Ordinary way, we must spend time dealing with the conflict that ensues. If we use "It's My Fault" and go the Exceptional route, we can often resolve the issue in just a few minutes or with minimal effort. We move through life with a lot less friction, stress and heaviness, and a lot more focus. We spend much less of our time fighting with others and more of it doing what matters to us. We contribute to our 25th hour.

Let me share one more story with you. In 2017, when I was CEO of the digital audio company Triton Digital, I travelled to London with my CFO, Mark, to meet with investors as part of our plan to go public on London's AIM stock exchange. One of the investor meetings was high stakes for us. If we messed it up, we would jeopardize our entire initial public offering (IPO). For several days before the meeting, Mark and I endlessly rehearsed our script and then rehearsed it some more. We plotted out everything we planned to say, and we agreed that we would *not* talk about certain topics that we felt would send the conversation in an unfavourable direction. If someone asked a question about those topics, we agreed that I would handle it, responding in a deft way that would keep the conversation on track.

When we got into the meeting, nobody asked any of the questions we'd feared – *whew*. But at one point, while addressing an entirely different topic, Mark brought up the topic we had wanted to avoid – entirely unprompted and in an offhand way. I nearly lost my shit. *WTF!* It was the biggest unforced error I'd ever seen.

Fortunately, I kept it together, and the meeting proceeded. Afterward, the attendees mingled, and Mark and I continued to chat with them. All along, I was stewing. I couldn't believe what Mark had done. His comment might have ruined everything.

Finally, when the last investor left the room and the door closed, I shot him a look that communicated what I was feeling. "Mark," I said.

Now, a person responding in an Ordinary way would have gone into defence mode, protesting that they hadn't done anything wrong or claiming that they had somehow felt they *had* to make that statement. Maybe they would have accused me of being oversensitive on this point, contending that raising the issue wasn't the big deal that I thought it was. But that wasn't what Mark did. Instead, he said, "Yes, Neal, I did that. If you need to yell at me or get it out, let's get it over with. But here's our choice: either we can talk about what I did, or we can talk about how we're going to fix it."

Mark's ability to rise above his defensive response stunned me. He acknowledged in a very clear way that he'd messed up. But he was right – we didn't need to talk about it. What mattered was fixing it. And so for the rest of that day, that was what we focused on. As it turned out, Mark's gaffe wasn't the big deal that both of us thought it was. Soon afterward, market conditions shifted, and we wound up deciding not to go public. Instead, we sold the company to private buyers, a decision that worked out for the best.

A few years afterward, Mark passed away, and his wife gave me the tremendous honour of eulogizing him. As I thought back on his life, this story was the first that jumped to mind. It occurred to me that Mark never did apologize for his mistake that day. He never said, "My goodness, I know we rehearsed. I'm so sorry. I feel terrible. I stepped in a pile of crap." Rather, he owned his mistake and then indicated his willingness to help pick up the pieces. That was all that was required of him. It was enough. I not only hadn't cared about his lack of apology; I hadn't even noticed.

This was a man who had mastered his defensive tendencies. He was secure in himself and not fearful, even when he knew that others were upset with him. He wasn't perfect, but he didn't have to be, nor did he feel compelled during difficult times to prove to himself or others that he was in the right. That maturity, that Exceptional ability to master his emotions and manage *himself*, not only made him unusually effective as a colleague and friend, it made him wonderful to be around and an inspiration for others around him.

I had once earned the nickname "Defensive". Mark had earned a very different and much more attractive moniker: "Exceptional". If you use "It's My Fault" – if you really take it to heart and practise it – maybe one day you'll earn this nickname, too.

Find Your 25th Hour: It's My Fault

For the next month, focus on the idea that everything is your fault. And I mean *everything*. A storm knocked out power to your house – it's your fault. There's traffic on the highway – it's your fault. The light bulb in your sister's lamp blew out – for sure that's your fault. Bring a new lightness to how you think about words such as "fault" and "blame". The more you can remove the stigma that these words carry, the easier it will be in real-life situations for you to behave in Exceptional ways.

Six

Turn Insults into Fuel

In January of my fifth-grade year, I got into a little tangle with my classmate Chris. It might have been more than a little tangle – I still remember it all these years later. I was the new kid in school, having transferred midyear. I was standing outside on the snow-covered playground during recess, wearing a nice, new coat my mother had bought me for the harsh Michigan winter. It was one of those big, puffy things with brightly coloured panels of red, orange and blue – very 1980s chic. Chris, who had pin-straight blond hair and braces on his teeth, approached me and, in full earshot of several other kids, said, "What kind of jacket is that? It looks so stupid and babyish."

My stomach tightened, and I reacted in the kind of Ordinary way you'd expect of a fifth grader. "It's not babyish," I said.

"It's the absolute dumbest jacket I've ever seen."

"You know what," I said, glancing around at the other kids, "you're an ass, obviously with no fashion sense. My jacket isn't so bad. Two of my buddies in my last school had the same one." That last part wasn't true – nobody I knew had that jacket.

I didn't usually behave that aggressively, but I was devastated to have been called out in front of all these other kids whom I had recently met. For the rest of that school day, I couldn't stop thinking about Chris's insult and whether my jacket was babyish. I continued to obsess about it that afternoon after I got home, glancing at the jacket hanging on its hook. By dinnertime, I had decided: there was no way in *hell* I was wearing that jacket to school again.

My parents begged to differ. They'd paid good money for the jacket, and my old one was too small. It was freezing outside, and I needed something warm. Like it or not, I was wearing it.

Uh, no – I wasn't. The next day, I left our house wearing my allegedly stupid and babyish jacket. But when I reached the bus stop, which was out of sight of my house, I removed the jacket, stuffed it into my backpack, and threw on a sweatshirt I'd brought with me. During the school day, when we went out for recess, I continued to wear only the sweatshirt. That wasn't ideal – I was shivering with cold. But it was better than looking like a loser in front of all the other kids. I continued that routine for the rest of the winter.

My solution worked far better than I could have imagined. The other kids saw me going out without a jacket, and they thought it was cool. They started copying me and before long were looking to me as the leader. When spring rolled around, I kicked Chris's butt in a kickball game at recess. My adjustment to my new school was complete.

The following year, I learned a much better way of handling situations when people insult you. Our teacher, Mrs Neuman, led us in a class discussion about bullying and how we might best respond. That was unusual; schools back then weren't sensitive to bullying as an issue. But Mrs Neuman had some great advice. As she noted, most people would respond to a bully the way I had: by pushing back. They would then waste time stewing about the insult they'd received, and they would enlist *other* people to help them feel better, wasting their time, too.

Mrs Neuman had a radical idea: instead of pushing back against Chris's bullying behaviour, I could *agree* with him, nodding my head and saying something such as "Yeah, my jacket is kind of colourful, and I can see why you'd find it babyish. But I've got to tell you, it's super warm." If I couldn't think of a way to agree, I could simply say, "Thank you for your feedback."

Agreeing with or thanking someone who insults you defuses the conflict. If I'd done that with Chris, our dispute would have been over. There wouldn't have been much more that Chris could have said. He wouldn't have had the satisfaction of tweaking me and getting an emotional response. He probably would have gone on to pick on someone else.

Mrs Neuman's advice for handling a bully would inspire a tool that I've used for years to help my clients save scads of time. Called "Turn Insults into Fuel", the tool crystallized for me while I was working with one of my first client companies. The head of sales, Isabella, was bullying Matt, who led operations. Upset that the company had shipped product late to one of her customers, Isabella went up to Matt and said, "Hey, your team was late again. You guys totally suck."

Matt reacted in an Ordinary way, which is to say, defensively and argumentatively. Feeling personally attacked, he said, "My team doesn't suck. It wasn't our fault. We did exactly what we were supposed to. *You're* the ones who aren't communicating the orders properly." To buttress his point, he ran report after report showing that he was right and she was wrong. It was a total time sink – and frankly, not all that different from how fifth-grade me had responded to Chris on the playground.

This kind of drama happens constantly in workplaces, exacting a terrible price. Workplace bullying costs companies hundreds of billions of dollars each year, dragging down productivity, loyalty, morale and more.[1] Rudeness is a massive time suck, with 80 per cent of workers who have experienced incivility reporting that they wasted time on the job perseverating over what had happened.[2] Managers also waste *their* time managing conflict; one study found that they were devoting over 10 per cent of their work schedules to picking up the pieces after incidences of rudeness.[3]

Channelling Mrs Neuman, I showed Matt that he could avoid responding negatively by agreeing with Isabella's gripe at least to some extent. "You're right," he could say to her. "The shipment was late, and that's not good." Bingo – the tension is defused. But he could also go a step further: he could look at the gripe Isabella had flung his way as motivation for him to take positive action. After all, he didn't want the shipments to be late any more than Isabella did. And he could take some satisfaction in proving that her insult was totally wrong.

Instead of arguing with her, running reports or, even worse, insulting her back and starting a feud, he could focus on diagnosing the problems and solving them. He could look at Isabella's gripe as containing some kernel of valuable feedback, albeit poorly communicated, and address it. He could turn her insult into *fuel* for his ongoing efforts to improve his performance – not only for her benefit but for his own and the company's.

"Turn Insults into Fuel" is a close cousin of "It's My Fault", in that both tools help us handle the negativity others spew at us. But an insult isn't the same as a mere criticism or assignment of blame. When someone insults us, they disrespect us or show contempt, conveying our worthlessness in their eyes. Insults can be especially derailing, distracting us and impeding us from pursuing our goals. Because humans have a "negativity bias", insults occupy our minds for longer than compliments.[4] We feel them viscerally, processing them as, in the words of some researchers, a "mini slap in the face".[5] Even small insults or microaggressions can unsettle us, making it harder for our brains to process ideas.[6]

"Turn Insults into Fuel" flips the script. We defeat bullies by becoming even *more* dedicated to our own and our team's success. We neutralize aggression and then take the righteous indignation we might feel and channel it into positive action. This has some science behind it. Research suggests that anger can serve as a productive force, motivating us to take positive action and enabling us to achieve our goals.[7] We see this happening in sports with the phenomenon of trash talk. Yelling "No way your lame ass can make that three-pointer!" while playing a game of pickup basketball often inspires your opponent to do their utmost to hit that crazy-ass shot.

We often think that the most reasonable and mature response when others insult us is to ignore it or let it go. But most of us don't *really* let go of an insult. Instead, we push down the anger and pain that we feel, pretending it doesn't exist. The insult gnaws at us, leading us to waste time and energy as we spiral over it. Our mental and physical health suffers.[8] We might also try to punish people who have behaved aggressively toward us, pulling away from them in a passive-aggressive way or working subtly to undermine them. Our performance declines, as does the team's.

It's more effective, I find, *not* to let insults go right away but to work with them in a way that helps us. Instead of allowing ourselves to feel wounded, we can heal ourselves by addressing the kernel of justified criticism that the insult might have contained, taking action to prove the bully in our life wrong. Instead of saying "I feel like shit" and then wallowing in that feeling while resolving to move on, we can think, "I'm going to *fix* this shit" – and then actually do it.

How I Became a *Much* Better Manager

To convey the potential of "Turn Insults into Fuel", let me tell you how I once used it to improve my own performance. Well, I *sort of* used it. That was years ago, back when I was practising the behaviours implied by "Turn Insults into Fuel" but not thinking of them as a tool per se. I was in my late twenties and working at Interep, serving as regional manager in our largest division. A number of teams were reporting in to me, and I was doing my best to be not merely a good manager but an Exceptional one. My best wasn't good enough, however. Nobody had sat me down and taught me how to manage people well, so I often didn't know what I didn't know.

One day, I had a chat with a star salesperson on a team that I oversaw. Her name was Tina, and she hadn't followed up with me on some tasks that she'd been assigned. When I asked her why, she uttered, without realizing it, one of the worst insults any employee could have thrown at me. "Well," she said, "you're intimidating." That might not sound like much of an insult, and I know that she didn't intend it that way. But at the time, it was devastating.

You see, I prided myself on being approachable, fair, kind – still do. I sincerely wanted to be an excellent manager who was there for others, and I worked hard every day to build strong, trusting relationships with my team members. I felt certain that, by and large, I was succeeding. The last thing I thought about myself was that I was unapproachable, overbearing or intimidating.

I responded to Tina's comment by getting defensive. And argumentative. Maybe a little angry. "What?" I said. "How am I intimidating?"

"You just are, Neal."

"But I always follow up with you. I check in with you. I call you all the time. I give you extra days off. I ask you about your kids. How is any of that intimidating?"

"It just is."

She wouldn't back off on her statement. But she also couldn't articulate what I was doing that left her feeling so intimidated. I found that horribly frustrating.

That encounter, which lasted only a few minutes, left me reeling. It's a good thing I wasn't doing "Credits and Debits" back then, because I would have been seriously in the hole. I could have agreed with her in the moment rather than pushing back. "Huh, interesting," I might have said. "Thanks for letting me know about that." What I did manage to do, despite my ingrained Ordinary behaviour, was to take Tina's comment seriously. She was one of my best performers and I didn't want to lose her, so I had little choice. If she felt intimidated, I must have been doing something that was leaving that impression. I would have to figure out what that was and then fix it. Without realizing it, I was treating her insult as fuel for my own growth as a manager.

I went on to have other conversations with Tina in which I asked for more feedback. I also embarked on an informal listening tour, asking other team members to have lunch with me and broaching the subject with them. "Hey," I said, "I won't reveal who said it, but it came up that I'm intimidating, and wow, that was so hurtful to me, because I pride myself on being very supportive and effective." I asked what their honest impressions were. If they likewise found me intimidating, I inquired precisely why.

Team members affirmed that they found me supportive and effective, but they also agreed with Tina. The reason was a huge eye-opener for me. Then as now, I took pride in my tendency to move quickly and get a lot done each day. That's no surprise, right? My team members reported that that could be off-putting. I'd race into their offices in the morning, skip past the niceties, and rattle off a quick series of questions: "Hey, what do you think about this strategy? How does that idea strike you? And what's happening on this account? What about on that account?" The intensity at which I worked made the team members feel as though they couldn't always keep up. Since I was the boss, they found me intimidating to be around. They worried that I expected them to operate at the same pace. What if they failed to keep up?

Now that I understood the problem, I worked to fix it. I slowed down with the team members, spending more time asking about their families and other personal interests. I tried to show more vulnerability myself, talking about my own life outside work. In short, I became warmer and gentler. I hadn't realized that team members needed that kind of personal touch from me or that having a more approachable boss would be motivating to them. Shifting my behaviour took months, but the impact was enormous. My relationships improved measurably. Tina in particular became much more comfortable around me, and her team's productivity soared.

This episode was a turning point in my evolution as a leader. After leaving Interep, I continued to work on my approachability as a leader, and I still work on it today. Understanding that my emphasis on speed and efficiency can rub people the wrong way, I make adjustments on a daily basis. When I visit companies, I always head into the break room trying to spot junior team members. I'll say hello and start a conversation, knowing this bit of rapport goes a long way. As a bonus, I wind up learning about their lives and how they see our business. It's a win-win all around – and a great payback for the couple of minutes that it costs me.

"Turn Insults into Fuel": A Closer Look

Analysing this example, we can break down "Turn Insults into Fuel" into a series of steps:

Step 1: Defuse the insult.

Do this by agreeing with it in some fashion. I skipped that step with Tina, but hey, I was young.

Step 2: Identify the growth or improvement opportunity.

This might be immediately obvious, as in Matt's case, or you might need to do some due diligence, as I did during those one-on-one lunches. Sometimes the insults you receive might be relatively trivial and won't spark a deeper change. Someone thinks your jacket is babyish – so what?

Step 3: Seize the opportunity.

This is the money step, where the insult really does become the fuel. Work hard to reverse subpar decisions, change processes and adopt healthier and more productive habits.

Step 4: Track your progress.

Are your actions having any impact? If possible or applicable, track actual performance data. At the very least, check in periodically with others to get their feedback.

Step 5: Keep the process going.

Matt needed to continue to work on his team's operations; it would have been a mistake to make just one round of improvements and stop there. And in my case, Tina's insult had cued me to some basic habits of mine that needed change. For the change to stick, I'd have to continue to work on it over an extended period and even try to deepen it.

At first you might find it hard to work with these five steps; the blow that the insult has dealt to your ego might feel too great. My guidance to you: keep practising. If a bully in your orbit insults you repeatedly, run through the steps each time in your mind to see if you can apply the tool more fully and take bolder and more concerted action. Think about the insult and its meaning, tallying up all the time you spend feeling upset and commiserating with others. Imagine the satisfaction you might get by taking action and showing your bully that when it comes to you and your worth, they're dead wrong.

It can help to deploy "Turn Insults into Fuel" in tandem with other tools covered in this book. In the moment, use "Pause Button" and

"Focal Point" to shake your brain free of the fight-or-flight response. You might also ask yourself what the person intended when spewing out an insult. Understanding that Tina's intent wasn't to hurt me made it easier for me to flip the script and look for ways to address her underlying concern. If a bully does intend to hurt you, you can ask yourself: What does that say about them? Do you need to feel hurt by what they said? Why do you care? As my clients find, the tools I present all flow together. As you master them, you'll be able to fall back on your favourites, and you'll also be able to call upon certain combinations that can help you address the situation at hand most effectively.

If "Turn Insults into Fuel" feels strange, it can help to remember all you have to gain by using it. If I hadn't been inclined to turn Tina's insult into fuel, I might never have made a critical change in my management style. I would have missed a massive opportunity. Without "Turn Insults into Fuel", Matt likewise might never have made valuable improvements to his team's operations.

The beauty of "Turn Insults into Fuel" is that it takes a difficult, painful moment and turns it into something potentially amazing. In essence, you learn to reframe an insult as useful feedback. Sometimes you can't see it that way; it might just be raw aggression, a middle finger raised in your direction. But many times, the kernel of feedback is there for you to unpack. The more you use "Turn Insults into Fuel", the more natural it will seem to see insults this way and to take decisive action. Not only will you save time you would have spent feeling terrible or engaging in tit-for-tat drama, you'll unleash tremendous energy for change.

It's always tempting to push back at bullies or withdraw from them. But we can do better by paying less attention to them and instead managing *ourselves*. What could you do with the time you might otherwise spend feeling hurt by a harsh remark that someone made? And what might you accomplish by forgoing the chance to prove that bully wrong?

Find Your 25th Hour: Turn Insults into Fuel

What is the most insulting thing anyone has ever said or done to you? Close your eyes and think about that for a moment. Maybe it was a comment someone made on the playground during grade school. Maybe it was a devastating remark an old flame made during your breakup. Maybe it was your best friend's failure to attend your wedding – with no good excuse – after RSVPing. Whatever the case, think about how you reacted. If you responded in an Ordinary way, were there any opportunities for growth that you squandered? What positive action might you have taken?

Go back in time and picture yourself in the same situation, only this time, apply your tools. How much time and heartache would you have saved? As you apply "Turn Insults into Fuel" in your daily life, keep this episode in mind as a negative inspiration.

Seven

When You're Suffering from a Case of the Ucks, Do This

Let's talk for a moment about you and, in particular, how awesome you are. If you stop to think about it, you really are quite amazing. You have a set of unique talents and skills, superpowers that allow you to kick some butt at work and in your personal relationships. Maybe it's your raw intelligence. Or your empathy. Or your ability to make friends with anyone. Or your decisiveness. Or how conscientious and organized you are. Are you perfect? Heck, no. But like any of us, you've got *a lot* going for you.

While we're at it, I'll bet your life also has some wonderful external aspects to it, even if, again, it's not perfect or if certain parts of it happen to be downright dreadful. Maybe you love your job – most of the time. Maybe you're a student and love your classes. Maybe you have a loving spouse whom you admire and trust. Maybe you get to enjoy fun times with your kids. Maybe you have a few cherished, lifelong friends whom you get to see regularly. Maybe you have a hobby that makes you feel good, week in and week out. Maybe you're in pretty good health for your age. Maybe you have a mentor who looks out for you or a neighbour who helps you out and brightens your day when you see them. Maybe you just saw a brilliant movie that changed how you look at the world.

Why am I the only one here thinking about all of this good stuff? You need to be doing that, too. Whoever you are and whatever your current circumstances, put down this book and take a few minutes to reflect on all the amazing parts of your life. Visualize yourself enjoying them. Reflect on how *grateful* you are for them. Tell yourself out loud that you're grateful.

Think, too, about parts of your life that aren't going so well. Can you identify some positive elements in them? Maybe you have a colleague whose behaviour is bugging the crap out of you but who is also extremely smart and a great contributor. Maybe your boss is demanding and difficult to be around but also, in the process, motivates you to work your hardest and to grow. Maybe your teenager is acting out but also bringing you and your spouse closer together as you figure out how to deal with it. Focus for just a moment on the positive sides of some challenging people or situations that ordinarily get you down. Think about how they might benefit you. Allow yourself to feel grateful for them for just a moment.

This exercise of pausing and feeling grateful is an important tool of mine, one that I call "Gratitude Equals Joy". In the crush of daily life, we often don't think of gratitude as a powerful strategy available to any of us to change our mood and outlook and to save large amounts of time in the process, but it truly is. Researchers in the discipline of positive psychology have found that experiencing or expressing gratitude can make us happier.[1] Simply offering thanks in writing for good stuff happening to us or penning a letter to someone telling them how grateful we are to them for doing us a good turn can leave us feeling happier for *weeks*. We walk away with a brighter view of our circumstances and future prospects. We give ourselves a huge boost of positive energy.

Gratitude is, as some have called it, a "mental health game

changer".[2] It alters our brains in detectable ways, leaving us less prone to anxiety and depression.[3] And it saves us all the time we would have wasted obsessing over our problems and feeling bad about them rather than being productive.

I use "Gratitude Equals Joy" to manage my moods, help myself feel better, and work toward a 25th hour. I live in Los Angeles and know many people whose lives were devastated by the 2025 wildfires. Thankfully, my family was spared – the worst I've had to deal with is a daily commute that is more than twice as long, thanks to some road closures caused by the fires. It's ridiculous for me to complain about the traffic, given the losses others have experienced. But if I'm honest, crawling forward at four miles per hour while others around me are blaring their horns really tears into my nerves and brings me down.

One day not long ago, I fought back with the power of gratitude. During a particularly rough morning when I sat in traffic for nearly two hours, I dashed off a text to my friend Todd, telling him how grateful I was to know him and feel connected to him. I expressed that the depth of trust we have between us is super important to me and that I felt appreciative of our friendship. I knew that I was going to be spending the rest of the day coaching and that others would be depending on me. I couldn't go into work feeling frustrated and unnerved, nor did I have time to waste spiralling over, ironically, how much time I'd just wasted. I wanted a hit of joy, and sending that text did the trick. For a moment I got to bask in the sunshine, which allowed me to recalibrate, feel better and set myself up for a great day.

"Gratitude Equals Joy" first crystallized during an engagement I had with a client named Marcus. Although only in his early thirties, he was the president of his family's very successful manufacturing business, which his father owned and had previously led. Marcus came to me because he was inexperienced as a leader and felt in over his head; he wanted to deal with his feelings of impostor syndrome.

Before long, a different problem cropped up – his father. Semiretired and in his seventies, Marcus's dad didn't want to be involved in the business very much. He trusted his son to make most decisions. Still, he had a habit of dropping into the office every few weeks without warning, popping into meetings unannounced and demanding to know what was going on.

Marcus knew that his dad was well within his rights to do this. As the company owner, he could do whatever he wanted. Still, Marcus deeply resented those intrusions. He valued his independence and felt that his dad was trying to control him and flex his own muscles as "the boss". The situation caused a great deal of tension between Marcus and his father, leading Marcus to waste untold amounts of time spiralling.

As I thought about that conflict, I noticed something: Marcus had been given a tremendous opportunity to run a successful company at such a young age, yet he didn't seem grateful for it. In fact, he didn't seem grateful for very much. He certainly never thanked me after our sessions together, nor did he ever seem to express gratitude for friends or other family members.

I thought back to when I had been Marcus's age. I hadn't worked for a family business, but I'd had three amazingly supportive bosses (including the one who'd called me defensive), and they'd all given me access to tremendous opportunities. Had I felt grateful enough? Yes, I think I had, but I'd never really expressed that emotion outwardly. Realizing that it wasn't too late, I texted each of them to tell them how meaningful it had been to work for them and how much I appreciated their support. Those individuals were all in their seventies and at a later stage in their careers, so you can imagine how nice it was for them to hear from me. I, too, came away feeling happy and joyful. And just like that, "Gratitude Equals Joy" was born.

Applying this tool with Marcus, I pointed out to him his apparent lack of gratitude and suggested that instead of wasting his time feeling angry at his dad, he would be better off expressing thanks to him for all that he'd given him. I urged him to give it a try. Marcus did, and as he reported back to me, it felt great. He loved his father and really did appreciate the opportunities he'd given him. His dad, meanwhile, was blown away that his son had thought to thank him. That, coupled with a well-timed use of "What's the Intent?", led Marcus to an epiphany. Contrary to what it might have seemed, his dad wasn't really trying to get in his way. At his age, what he wanted was to feel that he was still relevant. Given how much his dad had given him, Marcus was more than happy to help his father feel relevant by listening to his ideas, including him on certain projects, inviting him to meetings, and tolerating his dropping in unexpectedly.

Focusing on gratitude created a profound transformation for Marcus. He wasn't an emotionally expressive person, and he broke down in tears on one occasion while we were discussing his relationship with his father. When I asked him to explain what he was thinking and feeling, he told me that he knew his father wouldn't be around for many more years. He wanted to make the most of the time they had left, and to do that he really needed to accept his dad for who he was. "I don't want him to ever feel that he isn't relevant," Marcus told me. "If there's something I can do to help him feel good about himself, I want to do that." As Marcus realized, he would find deep joy in doing more for that person in his life who had given him so much.

Gratitude didn't entirely ease the tension between Marcus and his father. They were struggling with a more basic problem: how to take what had been a great father-son relationship and turn it into a professional one as well. The two would have to negotiate how to work together smoothly and productively, a process that would take time. But "Gratitude Equals Joy" did enable the two of them to understand each other better, and it saved Marcus considerable time that he might otherwise have wasted in being distracted with anger and resentment.

Today, when the two argue, Marcus can more quickly get his bearings by flipping himself back into gratitude mode.

Marcus has also made gratitude a practice throughout his life. Since he began using the tool, he has ended every one of our sessions by saying "Thank you". He started texting members of his team with small messages of appreciation. His team has become more productive, and Marcus himself reports being happier at work. Now, obviously, I can't prove that gratitude alone led to these beneficial results. But clearly it played an important role.

Manage Yourself, Not Others

"Gratitude Equals Joy" works on several levels to shift how you think about yourself and your circumstances. First, like other tools of mine, it pulls you out of the distress you might feel, freeing you up to do an emotional reset. Second, it takes that reset further by prompting you to focus on the positive instead of the negative. But I think there's a third, even more profound level on which the tool operates: it prompts you to redirect your attention away from other people and onto where it really belongs: *yourself.*

Becca, a twentysomething working at a boutique accounting firm, had a job that was wonderful in almost every respect. She was learning a lot and making a good salary, and she had excellent work-life balance. But she just couldn't stand having to collaborate with Marv, one of the firm's senior partners. The two of them worked closely together, and although Becca knew that Marv respected her, she found herself put off by the way he treated others. Marv was an extreme perfectionist, and when someone on the team made a minor mistake, he'd send an email to a large group of people painstakingly documenting the error and criticizing that person. Becca couldn't stand being around such an abusive, heavy-handed boss. "What frustrated me," she told me, "was that he was leading by fear, trying to make people so scared of making a mistake that they didn't do it anymore. That doesn't work."

Becca found Marv so irritating that even a brief encounter with him or an email was enough to trigger an hours-long cascade of negative thoughts. She began to procrastinate on certain projects because she knew she'd have to deal with him. Doubting that she could approach Marv without damaging her career, she felt powerless to improve the situation. But she also didn't see how she could continue working with him: she was becoming stressed out, angry and unhappy. Her only option, she thought, was to quit her otherwise perfect job and move to another company.

After Becca started to implement "Gratitude Equals Joy", she began seeing Marv in a new light. Previously, her mind had been fixed on him and behaviours she found annoying and hurtful. We all do this; when we're in a conflict with others, our first inclination is to blame the other person. *They're* the reason we're upset. In turn, we try to manage others so that they will behave differently. We try to "fix" them or convince them to fix themselves. Sometimes that might work, but more often, it proves futile and exhausting.

In using "Gratitude Equals Joy", Becca stopped trying to manage Marv in her mind. She focused on managing *herself* and her own emotional response. She was acknowledging that while she might not feel empowered to change Marv or his behaviours directly, the attitude she took shaped how she *experienced* him. By focusing on feeling more grateful, she could shift her attitude and see Marv's behaviour in a more positive light. That put her into a better place emotionally, helping her think more clearly and save time.

As Becca focused on managing herself instead of focusing on Marv's actions, she reflected on some benefits to being around him that she hadn't noticed before. Marv's behaviour, which remained as unreasonable and uncompromising as ever, was immensely useful to her as a negative example. It taught her how *not* to behave later in her career when she took on a leadership role. Also, Marv was constantly testing her and others on their team. Since she had managed to rise to the challenge so far, she felt more confident that she could handle anything that a future boss might throw at her.

Following my advice, Becca wrote "G = J", shorthand for "Gratitude Equals Joy", on a small, bright-coloured sticky note and posted it on her computer monitor. Whenever she received an annoying email from Marv, she glanced at the phrase and switched from irritation to gratitude, reminding herself that "this is just another learning moment and something that will teach me how to push through adversity". The more she practised that switch, the easier and more natural it became for her to notice negative feelings of any kind and move on.

Instead of spending hours stewing about Marv, Becca began to focus more intently on her work. She enjoyed her job much more and could perform better. She even found time to devote to other parts of the job she found rewarding, such as sitting with new hires and welcoming them into the company. "Gratitude Equals Joy" "opened me to activities that are important to our company's culture but that I didn't really think about before because I was under this dark storm cloud," Becca said. She didn't need to change the objective circumstances of her job to feel happier. Learning to manage herself made all the difference.

Focusing on managing ourselves instead of other people feeds into a core tool I teach clients: "Control the Controllables". We waste so much time trying to influence aspects of the outside world that are out of our control. We do this when we try to manage others, but we also do it more generally as we navigate obstacles in our path. To get to a 25th hour – and frankly, to create a smoother, more enjoyable path through life – we must step back from trying to control everything and instead focus on controlling what we *can* control, which is our own emotional reactions.

Not long ago, I sent myself a package using a major delivery service, and it didn't arrive at my home as expected. I started to panic; I needed something in that package for an upcoming business presentation. I started calling the local store where I had dropped off the package and then the company's national hotline, wasting time trying to get through. When I finally did, I wasn't very friendly to the customer service representative who answered the phone, and I ended the conversation by grumbling something about "never using the service ever again". I placed frantic calls to my assistant and my wife, enlisting them to help me solve the problem and in the process distracting them from what they were doing.

My behaviour was grounded in fear that I wouldn't be able to make my presentation as I'd hoped and that there would be consequences for my business.

My reaction, which was very Ordinary, didn't get me very far. Yelling at the customer service person wouldn't get my package delivered more quickly. If anything, it would frustrate them, leaving them less inspired to do their utmost to help me. I was trying to control something – the company's service – that was mainly beyond my grasp.

What I could control was my emotional reaction. If I'd focused on tamping down my panic by using "Gratitude Equals Joy" and other tools in this book, perhaps in combination with one another, I'd have treated the customer service person more politely. Maybe, in a calmer state, I'd have thought of a workaround that would have allowed me to give my presentation without the material in the package. In that case, I would have saved myself the time I'd spent frantically trying to get the package back, as well as whatever time my assistant and wife had spent thinking about my problem.

Those Dreaded Ucks

Some obstacles that crop up in everyday life and affect our moods are discrete, short-lived or circumstantial. Others, like Marcus's challenges with his father, are recurring. And then there are those times when we fall into a more generalized funk that saps our motivation. As I mentioned in the introduction, I have a name for this malaise that can take hold of even the most optimistic among us: the Ucks. "Uck," we say, "I have to have lunch with that annoying client today" or "Uck, I have to attend that meeting today" or "Uck, I have to make dinner again tonight." Sometimes a specific setback – such as an argument we had with someone or a disappointment at work, or an insult we perceive that someone lobbed at us – can set us off down a trail of negativity. Everything around us looks a little dimmer than it otherwise might, feels a little heavier. We move slower, waste time and get less done.

I like calling this lingering, totally unfun state of mind the "Ucks" because labelling it in this lighthearted way can help us break free of it. As my wife, Beth, reminds me, the name is doubly funny for me because it calls to mind an old friend of my parents, Dottie, who was a real Debbie Downer. She was nice enough and funny in her way, but she complained about *everything*, saying Uck-this and Uck-that. Imagine this small, spunky woman with short dark hair grousing about everything. It's pretty funny in its way. A while back, I began calling my sister "Dottie" after a conversation in which she had complained about something and even said "Uck" out loud. She hated the nickname at first, but it has since become an inside joke between us, a term of endearment that brings us joy.

All of us behave like Dottie at least some of the time. I don't think I've met a single person, regardless of how cheery or upbeat they appear, who doesn't toss off an occasional Uck. People we don't know or like might invite us to a wedding, and we say, "Uck, do I really have to go to that?" We need to spend an evening doing our taxes instead of going out with our friends, and that, too, yields an outburst of Ucks. But if we're not careful, we can get caught up in a whole, seemingly unending Fourth of July parade of Ucks, with one coming right after the other. Or if you prefer a different metaphor, we can become sucked down up to our necks into a terrible quicksand of Ucks that won't let us go.

But it gets worse. Remember how in chapter 3 I discussed how negative feelings we have toward others can become contagious and spread? Well, the Ucks spread, too. Your Ucks might seem to be your own business, but they influence others to develop a case of the Ucks as well. Others hear us Ucking around and start mimicking it. It's as simple as coming home from work, having your spouse ask you how your day was, and responding "My day sucked. My boss did this, my colleague did that." Negative, negative, negative. What mood will your spouse probably be in after a grumble fest like that? Probably a negative one.

We might even try to commiserate with others around us, sharing our malaise with them and asking them to validate our feelings. Of course, we don't *think* we're commiserating; we tell ourselves that we're collaborating productively. Yeah, right. Now we're not only wasting our time, we're wasting others' time as well by dragging them into our Ucks. This happens *all . . . the . . . time,* sometimes affecting entire groups of people. At college, a student starts whining about how boring a class is, how unmotivated they are to study. Soon ten other people in their circle are whining, too. Nobody is motivated to attend class, study or frankly do much of anything. Think of all the time these people are collectively wasting. Chances are, it's *way* more than a 25th hour.

If you have a case of the Ucks, here are three quick steps to follow to haul your butt out of it:

First, stop yourself from picking up the phone and calling or texting someone to commiserate about it. Don't do it! Don't perpetuate that negative contagion.

Second, give the funk you're in a name – tell yourself that you've got a nasty case of the Ucks. That alone can elicit a hint of a chuckle and make you feel better.

And third, use your tools to pull yourself more fully out of it, avoiding the nasty and negative drag that the Ucks exert.

When it comes to the third step, "Gratitude Equals Joy" is perfect, and that's because gratitude is the opposite of the Ucks. When we're mired in the Ucks, we see only the negative side of our situation; it's as if we're in a low-grade depression that influences our perception. Gratitude flips us back toward the positive side. We already started to feel lighthearted about the Ucks in step 2. Now we're peppering in some joy as well. That's a good one-two emotional punch. Soon those darn Ucks will be but a distant memory – all because you managed yourself and focused on controlling what you could control.

In talking about the Ucks, I'm by no means minimizing the reality of whatever less-than-ideal part of your life you're fixated on. You might well have bothersome obstacles and challenges to contend with. Maybe you really don't like those people who invited you to their wedding. Maybe taxes really are a pain to do. Maybe you really don't want to go to that meeting. But obsessing about it and griping about it to others won't get you anywhere. Use gratitude to manage yourself past this emotional response and then, when you're in a calmer, more rational state, decide what, if anything, you're going to do about it.

When obstacles crop up, there is usually some practical action we can take, whether it's stripping it out of our life or figuring out some workaround that makes it more palatable for us. Maybe you'll decide that you're not going to be friends with the couple who invited you to their wedding anymore, since you don't feel comfortable around them. Maybe you'll hire a professional to do your taxes for you because that task drags you down too much. And maybe you'll ask your boss to reassign you to a different account so that you don't have to attend the crappy meetings.

But you won't arrive at these kinds of solutions unless you manage your own emotions first and then spend some time thinking about why this part of your life is bothering you. Focusing on gratitude is an easy, effective and efficient way of putting yourself into the right frame of mind, so that you can solve problems rather than dwelling on them.

Fuelling Positive Contagion

The Ucks are a virus, and a nasty one at that. But the joy that comes from feeling grateful is contagious, too. It might not be as catching as negative feelings are; those spread with frightening speed. But if you really try to cultivate joy through gratitude, you can create some positive contagion, prompting others around you to feel more energized and joyful. That in turn will lead them to become more productive, so that they can move toward their 25th hour.

The easiest way to get positive vibes flowing is to express your own gratitude. The next time you're feeling thankful to someone, act on it. Take thirty seconds to send them a thank-you text, something like "I just wanted to tell you how much I appreciate you for spending fifteen minutes helping me with that project. Thank you!" The person who receives the text gets a boost of positive affirmation. That evening, when *their* spouse asks them how their day was, they just might tell them about that wonderful text their colleague sent them. Their spouse will get a hit of joy, which in turn might prompt them to say or do something positive for a third person.

Not long ago, Beth and I spent a weekend at the home of a couple with whom we're friendly. The city they live in is about forty minutes from the home of one of Beth's childhood friends, Gail. Beth had only occasionally spoken to Gail for many years, and she wasn't sure whether to reach out to her on that occasion and ask for a meetup.

To give Beth a boost, I told her how grateful I was for her tendency to be inviting and inclusive with others. Maybe that made an impression, maybe not. But she did call Gail and invited her and her boyfriend to come to dinner with us and the couple we were staying with. She and Gail had a wonderful time. Afterward, Gail sent Beth a text that said, "Thank you so much for pushing me out of my comfort zone. I wouldn't ordinarily drive forty minutes to have dinner, but I had such a great time with you and Neal, and I loved meeting your friends. I'm just so appreciative, and I love you." Beth in turn shared that text with the couple who were hosting us for the weekend, adding a bit of joy to their day. Everyone felt better than they had before because of the movement of gratitude and joy through our little social group. That's positive contagion for you.

Gratitude is so powerful in work situations. In chapter 5, I told you about a CFO named Ellie who found herself in an ongoing conflict with Nikki, the head of Human Resources, and used "It's My Fault" to transform their relationship. Afterward, Ellie began using "Gratitude Equals Joy" to pull not just herself out of the Ucks but Nikki, too. Ellie noticed that when the two of them met for an hour to discuss a business matter, they wasted the first thirty minutes griping and gossiping about the company's culture. The conversation would leave them deflated and unmotivated to do their actual work together.

To break free of that dynamic, Ellie started to say something such as "Hey, Nikki, I'm so appreciative that I get to collaborate with you. Let's skip our Uck party and go straight into getting stuff done." That was all it took – with just a bit of redirection, Ellie saved them both a half hour of productivity that would have been lost to commiseration. Nikki noticed what Ellie had done and started to do it in other meetings she attended, telling colleagues how much she appreciated them and their efforts. She also told Ellie how grateful she was for having cued her into the magic of being thankful. It's hard to measure how much time was saved by the individuals involved, but it was considerable.

It's not easy to feel grateful when you're worried or depressed over a challenge you face. It's even harder when you've sunk into a dastardly case of the Ucks. I get that. But I promise you, with a bit of mental effort on your part, you can do it. And the more you get into the habit of feeling grateful at odd moments, the easier it becomes. Soon you'll notice how much smoother life has become – not because problems no longer exist but because you're not letting yourself swirl about them for minutes, hours or days. You've moved past the Ordinary response and are behaving in an Exceptional way. As you snag your 25th hour, others will start to notice what a positive, upbeat and optimistic presence you have. And as you take your gratitude to the next level, expressing it outwardly, your good vibes will spread to them, too.

Find Your 25th Hour: Gratitude Equals Joy

Over the weekend when you have a few minutes, make a list of at least ten people in your life – close family members, friends, colleagues, mentors – for whom you feel grateful. Spend some time thinking about each one and why you appreciate having them in your life. Send each person a short text message expressing in just a few sentences how grateful you are for them, briefly explaining why. When you're done, do a quick mood check. Do you feel happier? Check yourself again after you've received responses from them. You just set the power of positive contagion into motion.

Eight

A Fail-Safe Way to Handle Disappointment and Rejection

The tools we've examined so far in part II move you toward a 25th hour by enabling you to manage yourself rather than pursue the futile and exhausting task of trying to manage others. Yet these strategies aren't foolproof. A painful setback can *still* send you spiralling. I'm not talking about a major life crisis, such as a death in the family, a frightening medical diagnosis or a natural disaster. Those fall into a whole other category of bad, and you might need a therapist to help you through the trauma and loss. I'm referring to the kinds of disappointments that your average overachiever *perceives* as the end of the world but really aren't. Maybe it's learning that you didn't get that job you really wanted or that the top three colleges on your list all rejected you or that your romantic partner wants to take a pause or that you didn't get that perfect house you bid on or that your boss passed you over for a promotion and chose a colleague instead.

Disappointments like these can set off an emotional storm, dealing a harsh blow to your ego while triggering your worst fears. The Devil, who thrills at a good storm, starts yapping at you, delivering messages such as "You're worthless, you're dumb, you suck at your job, nobody likes you, you're doomed, you'll never achieve your goals, you're a loser." Yes, that lame-ass Devil is thumping on his chest, cackling and whooping, reminding you of every doubt or anxiety he's ever pointed out to you. "You see?" he shouts. "I was right!"

Meanwhile, the rational, mature part of you – your Angel – appears to have vanished. You know on some level that the Devil isn't right; you can still faintly hear the Angel's kind, calming words. But because the Devil's searing voice is so strong, you take everything he says as the Truth, and no amount of reassuring talk from others can convince you otherwise. You become lost in the storm, unable to find your way out. It's akin to having a case of the Ucks, but on some pretty serious steroids.

This mental state of misery verging on despair is a problem in and of itself, maybe an even bigger one than the original disappointment, because it prevents you from moving forward. Although it might not seem like it, you have the power to recover from the setback or even come out farther ahead; others in similar situations do it all the time. But to make a comeback, you must think calmly and rationally, and you must feel motivated to act. Unfortunately, all you want to do right now is flop down on your bed and bury your head in a pillow. Meanwhile, the hours, days or even weeks are ticking by, shooting your "Credits and Debits" ledger to pieces.

So what can you do? How can you shake yourself free of the misery and switch your rational, problem-solving self back on?

Simple: you throw a party.

Assignment: Be Miserable

I'm talking, of course, about a very specific kind of party: a "Pity Party". I first came up with this tool many years ago while working with Isabella, a sales manager I mentioned in chapter 6. One weekday afternoon as we chatted on the phone, she told me she was having a tough day on account of something that had happened at work. She was stuck in a storm of negativity about her job and doubting herself as a professional – she couldn't work and she could barely think straight. She couldn't even get it together enough to use the tools I'd taught her.

Stepping back for a moment, I realized that we couldn't address an emotional storm like that in a rational way, using words. I wondered if I might have more success by taking a more experiential approach and having her fully give herself over to her emotions rather than trying to manage them. Isabella was a high-functioning, solutions-oriented, high-achieving kind of person. I suspected that if I encouraged her to wallow in her misery, she'd quickly become bored. She'd manage to see outside her emotions, put them behind her, and think more rationally.

I told Isabella that we would take a new tack. She was to set a timer, and for the next four hours, she was to throw a pity party for herself. As the minutes ticked away, she was to allow herself to be absolutely, positively *miserable*. She wasn't to use her tools at all. Rather, she could do whatever she tended to do when she was miserable. Maybe it was binge-watching reality TV. Or scrolling endless shopping sites on the web. Or curling up in a foetal position in bed and putting the pillow over her head. She was to perform an activity like that while thinking about how upset she was about what had happened at work. She was to think about every fear that her situation aroused, every resentment and frustration she felt. She wasn't to fight the Devil any longer. Rather, she was to let the Devil own her.

But here's the catch: those four hours were all she had to be miserable. The moment her timer dinged, signalling that her pity party was over, I expected her to snap out of it and use her tools to manage herself. She was also to text me to tell me that her pity party was over and to confirm that she was moving forward with her toolbox.

We both hung up, and I went about my day, taking phone calls and attending meetings. I was expecting to receive a text from Isabella at six in the evening, but to my surprise, my phone pinged at about five, a full hour before her exercise was supposed to end. She said that she'd wrapped up her pity party early. She was done feeling bad and was focused on moving forward, using her tools to manage her emotions.

I was happy that she felt better, but after that, I didn't think about "Pity Party" for a while. I am continuously inventing new tools as I work with clients on an individual basis. Some of them are so useful and broadly applicable that I introduce them to other clients, while others seem more idiosyncratic and not especially relevant beyond the situation at hand.

Several years later, though, I encountered another client – a senior leader at a large entertainment company named Susan – who was stuck in an emotional storm even more powerful than the one Isabella had encountered. Susan had some personal stuff happening, and meanwhile her boss was overbearing and overly taxing and overly dependent on her and all of it was just overwhelming. Like Isabella, Susan couldn't use her toolbox since her emotions were running too high. "You know," she said, "all I want to do is drink some root beers, eat junk food and get in bed while watching some crappy reality television."

That comment reminded me of Isabella's pity party. "Susan," I said, "here's what you're going to go do. You're going to go drink root beer, eat junk food and watch crappy television, and you're going to do it while lying in bed. For the next two hours, and for only two hours, you're going to go have the most unbelievably incredible pity party in the history of humankind."

"Two hours isn't enough," she said. "I need six. I need ten!"

We wound up settling on a five-hour pity party, after which she was to call me and we'd start her using her tools again. Once again, it took place on a workday, so Susan would be sacrificing valuable work time to wallow.

Like Isabella, Susan didn't complete the assignment – although to her Devil's credit, she did make it a good, solid four-plus hours. When we spoke afterward, she told me that she'd found it too hard to do absolutely nothing for so long. She wasn't built for it. Eventually, her inner drive and determination had overpowered everything her Devil was telling her. Ever since she'd proclaimed her pity party over, she'd flipped back into action mode. Thinking through her situation, she'd begun using her tools and strategizing how she'd handle her relationship with her boss in a way that would serve her interests. She would focus on managing herself instead of trying to manage her exhausting boss.

Since that episode with Susan, I've been using "Pity Party" much more regularly with clients. I'm not sure if there's any real science behind it, but what I *do* know, after seeing dozens of clients throw pity parties, is that it works – literally every time. And I think it will work for you.

After all, you're smart, emotionally balanced, high achieving and motivated to succeed. You're always seeking to work more efficiently and effectively to add time back into your day; that's why you bought a book about achieving a 25th hour. By temporarily indulging your Devil, you're mobilizing your built-in conscientiousness to fight back against the Devil. By allowing yourself to feel awful and giving yourself a defined timeline for doing so (no more than four or five hours), you can become more aware of your emotions and step outside them. You start checking your watch, saying "Okay, I have two hours left of my pity party", "I have ninety minutes left", and so on. All of a sudden, you're less focused on your problems and more focused on time. You're thinking in a practical, rational way – even if just a little. That in turn leads you back to your rational self. You can reset, start listening to your Angel again, and get back on track.

Leading Through Adversity

Although "Pity Party" is a seemingly straightforward tool, my clients find it extremely affirming and empowering, not to mention fun. One of them, Mitchell, is a young entrepreneur who was growing a successful web-based business in the sports industry. Founded in 2019, the business grew steadily at first. But by 2023, it was in serious trouble. Mitchell had raised millions of dollars from investors to hire people and scale up the business, preparing for a future growth in revenues. But despite his team's best efforts, the anticipated revenue growth hadn't happened. As a result, the company was losing money each month, with no end in sight. It became clear that Mitchell needed to make dramatic changes: cutting underperforming departments, paring back the workforce and shedding a layer of managers so that the business could streamline its operations. If he didn't act decisively, investors would flee and the business would go under.

Mitchell orchestrated three rounds of layoffs that year, ultimately cutting dozens of people, or about two-thirds of the workforce. Those layoffs were excruciating for the affected employees, but they were also hard on Mitchell. Not only did he know and like the employees, he'd personally attracted them to the company, selling them on the notion that they'd be creating something new and moving the industry forward. He felt terrible knowing that he'd have to disrupt their lives, even though they'd all worked hard and done their best.

Mitchell made it through the first two rounds without freaking out, but as it became clear that a third round would be necessary, he felt overwhelmed. Many of his remaining employees had been at the firm the longest and had been extremely loyal to him. In addition, he felt bad because he knew that, given the economics of the business, he'd needed to cut more people during the second round but hadn't had the guts to do so. Because he hadn't been honest with himself about what was required, he'd wasted his employees' time and held the company back. Now, as he faced the task of deciding exactly whom to lay off and whom to keep, the Devil kicked into overdrive, whispering into his ear that he was "a shitty entrepreneur", a "crappy leader", incapable of making the hard decisions – the list went on and on. Mitchell was paralysed: he didn't know how to move ahead.

Though I heard the desperation in his voice, I didn't tell him what personnel decisions to make. That was for him to decide – once he could think straight and use his tools to manage his emotions. Instead, I insisted that he stop what he was doing and throw a pity party. It was midafternoon when the conversation took place, but that didn't matter; he needed to leave work right away and do it. He'd have three hours to go home, drink some of his favourite beverage and sit there stewing in his emotions. He had my official permission to wallow in the narrative that he'd failed all of those people and was a horrible leader. At the end of those three hours, the party would be over. He'd stop beating himself up and start thinking about what he would need to do as an entrepreneur to best manage his company.

Mitchell's pity party lasted for only thirty minutes, maybe less. He went home, cracked open a hard kombucha, and paced back and forth around his backyard. He'd just started sipping on a second hard kombucha when he decided that he couldn't handle all the negativity and that his pity party was over. He was done stewing and ready to start acting. He realized that he'd been letting his emotions cloud his decision-making and that it needed to stop. He needed to snap back to reality and *lead*, because, as he put it, "As a business owner I have a job to do, and if I'm emotional and erratic, I'm not going to make the right choices."

The next morning, Mitchell showed up early at work, resolved to make tough decisions and move his company ahead. Now that he was thinking clearly, he remembered some wisdom his grandfather, one of his most important mentors, had given him. To run a business well, his grandfather had said, you need to approach it like a manager assembling a sports team. You must understand the organization's goals and needs: are you running a golf team, or a basketball team, or a polo club? Once you understand what you're trying to do, you then build up a roster of people accordingly and make other, supportive decisions. "You need to understand what those spots on the roster are," Mitchell said, "because that informs how big the team needs to be and how much money you need to keep it running."

Taking that logical approach, he considered where his business was headed in the months and years ahead and what specific operational capabilities it would need to succeed. With that clear in his mind, he created from scratch a roster of people he wanted on his team. In doing so, he forced himself to make some tough but necessary decisions about which existing employees to keep and which he'd need to lay off. His basic test was this: was a person so essential that he'd be willing to sign them to a five-year contract right now? If so, he'd keep them on the roster. If not, he'd say goodbye to them. Even if someone had been at the company for seven years and even if they were a strong performer, Mitchell would not keep them if their skills were no longer the right fit for the roster he was building.

Upon concluding the process, Mitchell realized that he'd have to say goodbye to a number of employees, including some of the most senior and longest tenured. Those were very tough calls to make, but it helped that he was calm, understood what he had to do, and had followed a logical, carefully considered process. He still felt sad, but he didn't harbour doubts or misgivings about his decisions. He could also explain to departing employees in a logical way why it was vital to the company's survival to pare back the workforce and why their specific skills package no longer fit.

As Mitchell looked back on that episode about a year later, it was clear that the third round of layoffs as well as the other operational changes he'd made had been the right strategic move. By the end of 2023, the company was able to turn a monthly profit. By 2024, it was generating a steady flow of cash that Mitchell and his team could invest to grow the business. With the company not merely surviving but thriving, Mitchell could start to think about the long-term picture and plan for years of solid growth.

Mitchell was also able to work on expanding his use of his tools outside work. He's become more thoughtful about his life goals, asking himself who he truly wants to be as a father, a husband and a man in the world – not just now but five years from now or ten. In short, solving what ailed his business has freed him up to start to reimagine his entire life, and even to take his first vacation in fifteen years. "Pity Party" is just one strategy contributing to his evolution, but as he will tell you, if he hadn't been able to make it through his emotional storm and make the right decisions for his business at a critical moment, he might well still be stuck and struggling – or worse.

We have it in us to get through many of the emotional flare-ups and crises that hit us. When we're able to tap our inner resources and get through to the other side, the sense of validation and empowerment is amazing. That's what I love most about "Pity Party": by using this fun tool, we prove to ourselves that we can manage ourselves, even in moments of peak adversity. And we can do it with a bit of levity, so that we're able to stop taking ourselves and our situations so seriously. We come out stronger and more confident, and that inspires us to use our tools even more in daily life to work toward a 25th hour. With "Pity Party" in hand, our greatest moments of adversity can fuel us toward even greater growth. Before we know it, our life isn't Ordinary any longer; it's Exceptional.

My Most Consequential Pity Party

Let's talk for a moment about how to work with "Pity Party". Depending on how deeply caught up you are in your emotional storm, you might want to set aside more or less time for it. Some pity parties can be quite short. In one instance, a client of mine, Tom, had an important board meeting coming up, but he was struggling. I gave him only one hour for a pity party. But it turned out that that was more than enough. After just fifteen minutes, he came back to me and said, "Okay, I get the point of this. I'm ready to move on."

If you have more time and are deeply upset, you might want to set aside most of a day for a pity party. Let it rip! Choose activities that will force you to be by yourself and wallow. What do *you* like to do when you're down? Doomscroll social media? Go online shopping and purchase unnecessary items? Crack open a beer and go fishing by yourself? Go to the driving range and hit ball after ball? Curl up into a foetal position on your comfy couch?

I have a confession to make: this book might not have been written had it not been for "Pity Party". When I first decided to write *The 25th Hour*, having been urged by multiple clients to do so, someone introduced me to a writing partner – I'll call her Ally – who would help me get my ideas down on paper. Because she came highly recommended by a trusted client and was a big name in her business, I decided to work with her without a formal contract in place. We started to work on the book together and made some nice progress.

Then, out of the blue, something crazy happened. It came to light that Ally had behaved unethically. The allegations were serious, and with negative publicity swirling around her, she cut me off – she stopped returning my phone calls and emails. I tried to get her to send me the materials we'd written together so far, as I didn't have any of the electronic files, but I had no luck. Months of work were lost.

At that point, I became totally deflated. The Devil on my shoulder started shouting "You see? This weird set of circumstances is a sign. You don't really have a book in you. Why did you even try? Don't write it. There's just no reason. Oh, and another thing: you're obviously incompetent. You've spent your career in business. You didn't think to sign a friggin' contract with her? You've also spent your career hiring people. How was it that you failed to spot the warning signs and steer clear of Ally? Now you've lost all the work you did with her. Look how much time you've wasted."

I allowed myself to get caught up in that maelstrom for far longer than I care to admit. Okay, fine, it was about two months. When yet another client emphatically told me that I *had* to write a book and share this toolbox, I realized I was stuck and needed a pity party to clear out my emotions. So I gave myself one. My family and I had gone away for the weekend, and I set aside four hours on one of the days to say goodbye to my wife and kids, take a walk by myself and be miserable.

Only minutes into my pity party, I started to get antsy. I kept looking at my watch, wondering, *Is it over yet?* Thirty minutes into it, I thought, *This is absolutely crazy that I'm sacrificing four hours of a weekend with my family to be miserable about something that I had no control over.* I asked myself if I really wanted to write this book, and I knew immediately that the answer was yes. *So, Neal,* I said to myself, *let's forget about all the hours you wasted. What's the plan to get it done?* I knew I would be having lunch the following week with someone who had experience in the publishing industry. I decided then and there to ask them to refer me to an agent and in turn a new writing partner. I rejoined my family and enjoyed the rest of the day with them. The rest is history.

Great things can happen for you, too, if you're able to face down moments of adversity and not get excessively derailed by them. These moments don't prove that you're a lousy, awful, incompetent person, despite what the Devil might tell you. Rather, they challenge you to look at yourself, make important changes, solve your immediate problems, and grow. The more efficiently you can get past your emotions to do this work, the sooner you'll put yourself onto a path to even greater success. Painful moments of disappointment probably seem like the worst time to throw a party. But if your goal is to manage yourself better so that you can thrive, actually, they're some of the best.

Find Your 25th Hour: Pity Party

Imagine yourself throwing a truly epic pity party. Picture many of the key elements, including the location, food, mood, weather, activities and so on. What are you wearing? Are you inside or outside? If you're watching TV, what show? If you're listening to music, what kind? If you're online, what are you doing? Consider what you are drinking. Is it a hot or cold beverage? And what are you eating? A sugary treat? Your favourite pizza? By thinking through as many of the details as possible in advance, you'll be prepared to use this tool when you need it. Just decide on the length of your pity party, and get started!

Part III

How to Take Risks and Turbocharge Your Growth

Staying focused and managing ourselves through adversity from day to day is great, but it's not enough. To truly adopt an Exceptional mindset, we must go deeper and consider ways that our habitual behaviours impede our long-term development. Are we taking risks so that we can grow? Are we accepting responsibility for getting stuff done? Are we leading others well, or are we micromanaging, hampering their progress and our own? Are we challenging ourselves to look at our emotions honestly and express ourselves clearly? When we make fear-based decisions or allow our emotions to determine our behaviour, we become stuck and can't progress toward our larger goals. Using the advanced tools in this section, we can dismantle our Ordinary mindsets even more, operating at maximum efficiency and saving time while moving ahead more swiftly in our careers. Working with the tools frees us to achieve the higher levels of success and fulfilment we desire.

Nine

Three Essential Tools for Confronting Your Fears

Have you fired yourself lately? It's a serious question – have you? If the answer is no, I'd like you to walk into your office or some other private space and close the door (taking this book with you, of course). Close your eyes and imagine that your boss has called you in for a conversation. Please, humour me. You really are sitting there across the table from them. Imagine them giving you a sombre look and saying "Thank you for coming in." Speak these words out loud, as if you're inhabiting your boss's character.

Now switch perspectives, imagining that you're you in this situation. "No problem," you might say to your phantom boss. "I'd love to know what this is about." Again, speak the words out loud, even if it feels weird or goofy.

Your boss sighs and looks you in the eye. "I've got some unfortunate news to deliver. We all greatly appreciate all the work you've done for the organization, but we've made the difficult decision to let you go."

How would you feel upon hearing your boss say this? Maybe your heart would start to race. You'd break out in a cold sweat. "I'm surprised to hear that," you might say. "I've really loved working here. And I thought that I was performing well."

Switch back to your boss. "Listen, you didn't do anything wrong, and we really do appreciate your service. But we've decided to go in a different direction. Look, let's not make this difficult. We want to part amicably. We're going to respect your contract and pay you severance, but we've already found someone to replace you."

Spin out this conversation a bit more, imagining how, in your worst nightmare, your boss would deliver this news. Really try to capture your boss's character, down to their tone of voice, the precise words they'd use, how they would sit in their chair, any other body language they would use. Linger on the visual of them sitting there in as much detail as you can muster. And think carefully about how you would behave. Would you blow a gasket? Would you sit there calmly without saying much? Would you ask lots of questions? Would you cry? What would the experience *feel* like?

Now imagine the aftermath of this conversation. If you had to tell your significant other and close family members the news, how would that go? How would you break it to your kids, relatives and friends? Try to walk through those conversations as best you can. Think, too, about how you would pay your bills as well as other steps you would take in the short term to get yourself back on your feet.

This exercise, which I call "Fire Yourself", might take five or six minutes to do. If you're like my clients, you'll find it to be a real eye-opener, a boon to your efforts to learn and grow, and another valuable pathway to a 25th hour. It helps you manage your fears so that you can save time and perform at your best, rather than letting your emotions run wild or relying on someone else for reassurance.

Most of us stuck in Ordinary-land prevent ourselves from making bold, potentially beneficial career moves because we're riddled with underlying fears and don't know how to manage them. The vast majority of what our Devil blabs to us is fear based. One survey found that almost 90 per cent of workers were afflicted by fears on the job, while sizeable minorities reported that their fears had held them back from scoring promotions or pay raises.[1] We're scared of so much, whether it's speaking up at meetings, making errors on the job, or alienating our fellow team members. But the greatest fear of all by a wide margin is being laid off or fired. Another survey found that more than 50 per cent of people feared getting axed, with almost all of them reporting that they dreaded it "more than death".[2]

The fear of losing our job is usually irrational and way off base – but still hauntingly real and quite debilitating. When I was in my late thirties and serving as the CEO of Triton, which, as you'll remember, provides technology infrastructure for digital audio and podcast publishers, I was *terrified* that our lead investor and board member would haul me into a meeting and tell me that they no longer needed my services. It didn't matter that I'd founded the company, that we were creating value, that the board had said nothing at all to indicate its displeasure, and that I had no other data of any kind to suggest that my job was in jeopardy. My fear was all in my head, linked to the fact that it was my first significant CEO role, I felt insecure about my abilities, and I saw myself as an impostor. It didn't help that, like most CEOs, I received scant feedback, so I had trouble gauging objectively how I was doing. I thought I might be doing okay, but I didn't *know* that, and so my mind buzzed with a constant background dread.

Because I was so caught up in fear, I was behaving in Ordinary ways. During conversations with board members, my fears inhibited me, prompting me to try to constantly put on a good face. When challenges arose, I avoided saying or doing anything that would spark conflict – I was too scared. As a result, I failed to handle issues decisively, and they festered. Meanwhile, the swirl of fear distracted me, making it harder to think deeply about the business and enjoy time with my wife and three young kids. Every day, I piddled away my 25th hour because of that unfounded, irrational fear.

Realizing that I was struggling, I got the idea of confronting my fear once and for all by firing myself. I performed the exercise I just described to you, saying the speaking parts out loud. Did it feel uncomfortable? Yes. If someone had spotted me doing that, they would have thought I was silly. But it worked.

The theory behind "Fire Yourself" is like that of "Pity Party": instead of fighting the Devil, you give in to it and see what that feels like. Many of us try to ignore our fear or pretend it doesn't exist, but "Fire Yourself" prompts you to lean aggressively *into* it. As my clients and I have found, the very act of doing so wakes up the Angel. You can't linger very long in imagining your firing before you start to rally. You tell yourself, *Yes, maybe I'll get fired, but that's fine, because I'm going to figure it out. I'll get another job. I'll start another company. Life will go on. Everything will be okay.* And then you find yourself thinking about what your next practical step might be. Instead of staying stuck, you're back in the mode of getting shit done.

The Power of a Worst-Case Scenario

As helpful as it was to fire myself, I was so overcome by fear that I devised a second tool called "What's the Worst Thing That Can Happen?". In this tool, we defeat an irrational fear not by immersing ourselves in it but by using rational argument to overpower it. If we take a moment to fully appreciate just how ridiculous our fears are, we can often free ourselves of them enough to start behaving in an Exceptional way.

"What's the Worst Thing That Can Happen?" breaks down into two steps. First, as the name suggests, consider what the very worst potential outcome of your present situation might be. Is it that you'll fail? That you'll disappoint someone or lose them as a client or friend? That you'll embarrass yourself publicly? That you'll be fired, lose your house, break up with your romantic partner and not know what to do with yourself?

Take some time to unravel the stream of potential consequences that represents the absolute worst-case scenario in your situation. If you do, you'll usually find that the supposed nightmare isn't as bad as you're making it out to be. Sure, it's a setback or a disappointment, it might sting and it might inconvenience you for a time. But it's not a life-altering catastrophe – not even close.

Now proceed to step 2. Ask yourself: from an objective standpoint, what's the *likelihood* that this worst potential outcome will come to pass? When you really think about it, does it have a greater than 80 per cent chance of happening? Or are the odds more like 10 per cent or less? Be realistic, mobilizing as much tangible evidence as you can to make your assessment.

Almost always, my clients find that the odds of their worst-case scenario materializing are small – almost always well below 10 per cent, typically in the 1 to 2 per cent range, and sometimes even zero. It can come as quite a surprise to realize that an outcome that seemed so terrifying is in truth pretty remote. They've been worrying about something that not only is not that big of a deal but that almost certainly won't happen! Any number of asteroids whizzing by in space have non-zero but minute risks of hitting the earth. Do you worry about those? So why worry about your nightmare?

When I ran through the exercise as a young CEO, I concluded that the worst thing that could happen to me if the board fired me was that I'd be out of work with a family to support and have to find another job. That would suck. It would be an embarrassing failure that I'd need to explain to friends and family, as well as a financial setback in the short term for my family. It would be a big emotional loss for me, too. As Triton's cofounder and CEO, I'd put my heart and soul into the company and had a real passion for it. But I also knew I was young and talented, and I'd amassed a ton of valuable skills and experience. It wouldn't be long before I'd find another opportunity that I might wind up loving, too. Maybe I'd even start another company of my own. Being fired would be a setback, but not some kind of epic, irreversible disaster.

When I asked myself to assess the odds that I'd be fired, the picture seemed brighter still. First, I listed the expectations that board members had of me: they wanted me to drive revenues, operate the business well, develop new products and strategy, and so on. In general, I was doing well on all of these fronts. I considered if there were any specific issues – a subpar decision I'd made, for instance – that might have caused the board members to question my leadership. Further, I considered whether any of those mistakes on my part had been so serious, from the board's perspective, that they'd want to replace me. I drew a blank; there were literally no significant blemishes on my record. The only thing I could think of was that I'd hired a CFO a couple of years before who hadn't worked out. But even there, I'd managed to fix the situation by letting that executive go and hiring Mark, the amazingly Exceptional leader whom I described in chapter 6. There was a 0 per cent chance that the board would fire me for a single mistaken hire that I'd remedied and that hadn't caused issues for the company.

Although my analysis wasn't a quantitative one, I wanted to come up with a number to express my odds of being fired. I ballparked it at 5 per cent, knowing that even that was an inflated figure. I performed a little thought experiment: if someone approached me with two investment opportunities, one that had a 95 per cent chance of succeeding and one that had only a 5 per cent chance, to which one would I allocate my time, energy and money? It was obvious: I'd spend *zero* time and effort on the 5 per cent scenario and pour everything I had into the one that was almost certain to succeed.

When I thought of it that way, my Angel really kicked in. It would be silly for me to spend even a minute worrying about being fired. It just wasn't going to happen. And even if by some bizarre set of circumstances it did, it would take months or years for my company to let me go; there was a whole process that had to occur. I'd have time to prepare myself and maybe even mitigate my situation. All told, it made much more sense to forget about being fired and focus on what mattered most to me: leading my company and being there for my family.

"What's the Worst Thing That Can Happen?" didn't suddenly turn me into a fear-free leader. But it dealt a heavy blow to my Devil. Take that, you fool! Afterward, whenever I found my fear of being fired rising up, I reminded myself how unlikely it was to happen, putting it into perspective by running through that thought experiment about investing again. That mental strategy almost always took the air out of my budding fears, enabling me to refocus and quickly get back on track. Afterward, I loved calculating how much time and energy I'd saved by not allowing my Devil to erode my 25th hour.

Prepare Less and Do *Better*

In unpacking these two tools, I've considered a situation in which a senior leader was worried about being fired. But you can use "What's the Worst Thing That Can Happen?" with a range of fears you might encounter in your professional and personal development, whether it's alienating your new boss, messing up a client presentation, being rejected when asking a romantic interest out on a date, being passed over for a big promotion you wanted, or failing to get into one of your top colleges. In any scenario where you're striving for a goal and taking risks and irrational fears are bubbling up, I think you'll find that running through the two steps will lead to immediate time savings and better performance. It's also fun to calculate the percentages and realize that you're doing a great job using your tools!

Not long ago, a client of mine, the young CEO of a startup, called to ask if we could talk for a moment. He and his team were scrambling to prepare for a big board meeting the next day. They had just put in six hours of prep time and needed at least six more to feel prepared. He wanted to know: what could he do to make sure that they were energized and not exhausted the next day? My response: "Send everyone home right now." He protested that that would be counter-productive; he and his team needed to prepare. "Listen," I said, "do you trust your team?"

"I fucking love my team."

"Then send them home right now."

"Why? Our board meeting will be terrible."

"No, it won't."

I challenged him to instruct his team not to look at or think about work until 9:00 the following morning. Fifteen minutes before the board meeting, they were to convene and make sure they all understood the talking points and were agreed on them.

"You're insane," he said.

"Just try it. What's the worst thing that could happen?"

"We mess up, and the board members say that we weren't prepared."

"What's the chances that that will happen?"

He thought about it. "Maybe three per cent."

"So do you want to make a choice based on something that's only three per cent likely to happen or ninety-seven per cent?"

"Fuck – I get it."

"Great," I said.

He wound up doing exactly what I proposed. The next day, I got a text from him that read, "Best board meeting ever. It was unbelievable how we delivered it, and we were sharp as ever."

When it comes to board meetings and other important encounters, people tend to rehearse obsessively, only to achieve mediocre results. I've found that the same applies to overpreparing for a test or school project. Most of that preparation is unnecessary and counter-productive. We already know the material. We're well prepared. Yet our fears get the better of us, so we waste time and energy preparing. "What's the Worst Thing That Can Happen?" can help us cut through all that, allowing us to trust ourselves and others more to get the job done.

Fears also hobble us when we've embarked on a job search. Kelly, a young professional I coach, was unhappy with the finance job she'd taken out of college and wanted to move into the fashion industry. As she began interviewing, she became obsessed with landing a job at a certain big cosmetics brand. The company put her through an ungodly number of interviews, and before each one, she became anxious and spent many hours overpreparing. She became so stressed out and so fearful that she wouldn't get the job that she stopped interviewing anywhere else – she just didn't have the energy.

She didn't get the job. The problem, the hiring manager told her, wasn't that she lacked talent or relevant experience; it was that she wasn't a good "cultural fit". Her anxiety had shone through in her interviews, affecting how she came across to people at the company. She had literally worried herself out of a job.

It was a tough blow, but Kelly was determined to overcome her anxiety and land a job elsewhere. She lined up an opportunity at a top apparel company. Before going in for a round of interviews, we sat down to talk.

"Are you scared?" I asked her.

"Yep," she said. "Big time."

"Well, what's the worst thing that can happen?"

She paused to think about it. "Neal, I really like this company, but I also have four other potential opportunities that I'm working on. The worst thing that can happen is I don't get this job and I keep interviewing and I don't get those jobs, either."

"What's the odds of that happening? Be realistic here. Your résumé is super strong. You've got great experience, a great academic record and wonderful recommendations from your previous managers. You're smart. You're personable. You've been networking."

Again, she thought about it. "You're right, I do have a lot going for me. I put the chances that I'll get *some* job at greater than ninety per cent."

"So what, ninety-three per cent?"

"Sure."

Stepping back and thinking about her situation in a rational way helped calm Kelly down, preventing her fears from getting the better of her. Although she spent much less time preparing for the next round of interviews than she had for the earlier one, she wound up doing much better – and landing a prime job. The experience she brought to the table hadn't changed. But she wasn't overcome by fear and was able to project excitement and confidence. And people noticed.

Having Fun with Our Fears

While working with these first two tools with clients, I typically introduce them to another little strategy of mine – think of it as a bonus tool – to add in some levity. Our fears are serious business, but we can manage them better if we learn to laugh at them a little bit. My strategy for that is called "Fire Your Fears". Yes, there's more firing going on, but this time it's you in the driver's seat showing your lame-ass fears the door.

Go back into that private room with the door closed and address your fears out loud as if they were a real person. Explain to your fears that they're not needed anymore and that you've decided to go in another direction. Say something such as "Fears, you're really overwhelming me, and I've allowed you to do that up until now. But I'm going to start managing myself better, so your services are no longer needed. You're irrelevant to my life. I no longer want you in my head, dragging me down. I hate to break it to you . . . but you're fired!" You can also make your monologue more specific, saying something such as "Fear of public speaking – you're fired. Pack up all of your belongings, including the narrative of how I am not good at it, how I depend on a teleprompter and how my voice cracks. Get the hell out of my life. And close the door on your way out!"

If multiple fears are bogging you down, run through a separate firing scene for each of them. When you're finished, remind yourself that since you fired those fears, they're no longer present or available to disrupt you. Good riddance!

Some of my clients look at me funny when I assign this exercise, but they always report that they found it fun and enjoyable once they got past the initial awkwardness. When their fears return, as they inevitably do, I tell them that it looks as though their fears didn't really get fired; they've showed back up at the office. Speaking about it in this lighthearted way helps keep my clients from getting down on themselves for falling back into the same unhealthy mental patterns. Yes, they've fallen prey to irrational fears, but they don't waste a minute sweating it. Instead, they just fire their fears all over again and move on. And even that becomes lighthearted. "Listen, you distracting pain," my clients might say, "I just fired you, but you didn't listen. Get out! I'm serious this time! I'm calling security!"

If firing your fears sounds too outlandish, play with it a little. One of my clients just couldn't get into "Fire Your Fears", so instead he decided to send his fears on a vacation. His fears had to put an out-of-office message on their emails saying "Sorry, not available, I'll answer you when I get back." Somehow, for reasons I don't understand, that did the trick. Keep it light. Keep it fun. But make it clear to your fears: business as usual is over. There's a new sheriff in town. And it's *you*.

To make this tool even more fun, you might try incorporating an object that personifies your fears. Some of my clients create an image of their Devil and address that while they're firing their fears. They might print a picture of a Devil off the internet, complete with horns and red skin. One of them repurposed a picture of her much-hated ex-boyfriend as a stand-in for her Devil and her fears. Could you use a picture of a political leader you despise or a TV character you find totally annoying? Maybe. As my clients fire their fears, they crumple or tear up the picture of their Devil and throw it into the trash. This symbolic gesture cements the rejection of fear in their minds. As they tell me, there's something very gratifying about being about to physically destroy an image of the Devil who has been whispering fears in their ears for so long.

Like the other two tools in this chapter, "Fire Your Fears" isn't for everyone. If your fears are debilitating to the point where they prevent you from getting out of bed in the morning and participating in your usual activities, you might have clinical anxiety and need the help of a mental health professional. But if you're functioning well enough but find yourself hampered by irrational fears more than you'd like, I encourage you to give these tools a try. Most of us haven't tried to manage our fears. In fact, we might not even have acknowledged that we have them. The more we learn to do so, the more we can lean into our own long-term development. And the more fulfilling, enjoyable and successful our lives will become.

Find Your 25th Hour: Fire Your Fears

Make a list of your biggest professional fears – maybe it's getting fired, becoming obsolete thanks to AI, pissing off a big client or alienating your boss. Go through the exercise of determining how probable it is that the fear will materialize. When you've calculated the odds, determine the worst thing that could happen. Mustering all the data at your disposal, fire your fears one by one. Doesn't it feel amazing?

Ten

The Robot Is Your Enemy

Earlier in this book, I talked about how to use the "10 Per Cent Meeting Rule" and "Quick Check-in" to tighten up meetings, save time and frankly restore a bit of sanity to our organizations. Since meetings are such an intractable problem for so many, I'd like to return to the subject, getting to one of the core reasons why these gatherings are so freaking *awful.*

Years ago, when I first started my coaching practice, I noticed a striking pattern: a great deal of the way people behaved at work tended to be rote or preprogrammed. Regardless of the organization or industry, they tended to know the unwritten rules of conduct and stick to them without thinking. They were immersed in what we might call the culture of their workplace, locked into behaviours that everybody had embraced and come to expect as "normal".

I had three very different clients at the time: a marketing firm, a technology company and a startup. At the marketing firm, which had about sixty employees, everyone showed up for work at 8:00 am. At 8:15, they all gathered for an informal check-in meeting that lasted about an hour. Then they worked. At noon, they stopped for lunch. Some employees ate together – the same group every day. Work resumed at 1:00 pm. Around 3:00 pm, employees gathered in the staff kitchen for an informal snack. By 5:30 pm, everyone had gone home.

Every day, it was the same pattern. Heaven forbid that anyone ever decided to do something new – say, skip the 8:15 meeting or eat lunch at one instead of noon. I interacted with that firm for months, and nobody ever deviated from those norms.

At the technology company, the behaviours were different, but the routine nature of the workday was very much the same: People came in at nine in the morning and beelined for their desks. They put their headphones on and didn't speak to one another. No banter, no chit-chat. The company catered lunch, so at precisely 12:30 they all got their food, trucked it back to their desks, plugged their headphones back in and chowed it while continuing to stare at their screens. Again, that never changed. People were too locked into their routines.

If there was any workplace in which I wouldn't have expected preprogrammed behaviour to appear, it was the startup. As anyone who has worked in a startup knows, the environment is usually chaotic. Everybody is doing everything. Crises are constantly cropping up that need to be solved. There's a flurry of activity, an intensity – total craziness and a lack of predictability. But as I observed that startup, it hit me: the chaos was *itself* preprogrammed. It, too, never changed. It's not as though there were periods of calm, measured behaviour followed by explosions of frenzied activity. No; it was constant chaos. People had become used to racing around and collaborating informally and shouting back and forth across the room and all the rest of it. And they engaged in that preprogrammed behaviour without giving it a moment's thought.

So what does the routinized nature of work have to do with meetings? *Everything.*

Let's go back to that informal 8:15 meeting at the marketing firm. It usually lasted for about an hour, and during that time people talked about, well, absolutely nothing. Early in the company's history, when there had been only a handful of employees, that meeting had been useful. But now, as the company had evolved and grown, it had become a waste of time. Yet because of the robotic nature of workplace behaviour, the leaders had kept the meeting intact. It seemed sacrilegious *not* to have the meeting. It was "what we always did" – and nobody questioned it. Day after day, employees sat there with pained boredom stamped all over their faces as the group went through the motions. Since all sixty employees attended, that amounted to sixty minutes of lost productivity per employee per day. Over a year, assuming fifty workweeks, that was *fifteen thousand* hours of lost time.

Because of a single unnecessary daily meeting.

Breaking the Sequence

If you lead a team, ask yourself: are your meetings necessary? Or are you holding them simply because you or others are on autopilot, locked into a routine? Even if a meeting you organize is useful, does every part of that meeting or the way it's structured serve a purpose, or do you run the gathering that way "just because"? And what other aspects of life in your organization tend to be rote or routinized? Would changing a policy or a practice increase productivity or have other benefits?

One of the most helpful tools I teach leaders is one of the simplest. It's called "Breaking the Sequence". When completing any work task, big or small, don't merely make an incremental change; do it differently. Break the sequence. Look at it as an experiment. See what happens.

At the marketing firm, I'm happy to say, we broke the sequence when it came to those useless 8:15 meetings. Instead of holding them every day, leaders limited them to once a week. They changed up the agenda and, most critically, made them no more than thirty minutes long. Employees loved it. They saved all the time they'd been wasting every morning, and the weekly meetings they did have were enormously productive. Leaders also broke the sequence by experimenting with holding the weekly meetings on different days of the week – first on Monday, then on Tuesday, then on Wednesday.

Messing with the meeting might have seemed like a relatively minor change, and on one level it was. But it had broader implications. By removing the vast majority of the meetings, the company made time at work a bit less structured. Employees started to deviate from other work patterns they had set for themselves. They became more focused on doing what was productive rather than blindly hewing to established patterns. Instead of leaving at five on the dot every day, they started staying until seven or eight some evenings if they needed to finish a big project. Other days, when they'd accomplished their tasks, they knocked off a little earlier. They felt that they had more autonomy and that the leaders trusted them more. All because we'd broken the sequence in one highly visible way.

There are a million ways leaders can break the sequence in group settings. If you're a supervisor and you normally dominate team meetings, devote half the time to going around the room and asking team members to describe the most important accomplishment they made in their work the past week. Or here's another one: what if without any notice you ask participants at your next leadership team meeting to summarize the update that the person sitting to their right had given the previous week? One client of mine, who headed an investment firm, did precisely that. It made team members uncomfortable, but it prompted them to pay more attention to what their colleagues were saying and to chime in with creative ideas for them. The productivity of the meetings went through the roof, and they took only half as much time as they previously had.

If you're a top executive, try deploying "Breaking the Sequence" to fundamentally transform your business. I did, and the results were spectacular. In 2015, I became convinced that my company of 350 employees was wildly inefficient. The usual way of solving the problem is to consider each individual job and assess how to squeeze the most productivity out of the person performing it. That takes time, and it usually doesn't produce earthshaking results. Recognizing that we had too many managers bogging down work processes, I decided to break the sequence and bring about radical change. In a matter of months, we laid off approximately 25 per cent of our workforce. I told our employees, "We're removing the managers who have been serving as bottlenecks. It's up to you to redesign your work accordingly so that it's more efficient." On one level, it was an act of trust on my part, reflecting the progress I'd made in managing my own fears. I wasn't telling our people how to do their work; they would have to determine that themselves.

"Breaking the Sequence" was a godsend, unleashing incredible creativity among our workforce. We accomplished more in a few months than we might have in years by using a more incremental approach, implementing new procedures that no other tech company in our space at the time had tried. Our productivity soared. After some initial anxiety, our workforce loved it. With more autonomy, employees started to feel a new sense of importance and empowerment. My decision to break the sequence prompted me to challenge *everyone* in the company to break their own sequence. They became more engaged and bolder as a result, and they spread their enthusiasm to others. We became an organization of bold, curious people who moved more quickly and took responsibility for improving how they worked. Pretty cool!

In any organization, norms and habits are important. We need unwritten rules to ensure that members of a group coordinate their actions to get shit done. These rules can also give rise to a sense of camaraderie and common identity, which makes the work we do more fun and meaningful. But if we're not careful, the rules that inform group work can hurt, not help. As we lose sight of their purpose, they become millstones around our neck – something we do unthinkingly because we feel we must and because we're afraid of breaking with the status quo. Before we know it, we're wasting insane amounts of time and our creativity is flagging. The solution is to prevent rules from becoming too deeply entrenched. That's where "Breaking the Sequence" comes in. If you practise it often with your team, you can prevent work from getting stale, and you can adapt better to changes in your business or industry. Your entire team moves toward a 25th hour.

Your Own Personal Robot

For those of us who don't lead a team, "Breaking the Sequence" is still one of the most useful tools in our toolbox. Anyone can use it to accelerate their own long-term growth and development by managing themselves better and behaving in ways that are more emotionally mature or Exceptional. That's because it's not just groups of people that behave robotically together. It's individuals. It's *you*.

Think back to grade school. To progress from first to second grade, you had to meet some basic criteria – for instance, develop basic maths and English skills. To get to third grade, it was a similar story: There were criteria you needed to meet, and you worked all year to get there. This process of working to achieve performance benchmarks and proceeding stepwise continued year after year during elementary school and on into middle school. In high school, you had more flexibility, but you still had to run through a long series of well-defined hoops to get into the college of your choice. In college, you had to do it all over again to get a good job.

Day after day, this process of striving after goals translated into a predictable schedule. During your school years, if you were like me and my friends, you woke up, had breakfast, went to school, played your sport or engaged in your after-school activity, came home, did your homework, went to sleep. Then you did it all again. And again. And again. School itself was robotic. In Michigan, where I grew up, we lined up single file during the elementary grades to go outside to recess. Every day. We took precisely the same route down the hallway and out the door. When we came back in, we again lined up single file outside in the playground and retraced our steps. In middle school, we had the same classes every day and at the same times. In high school, we rotated classes; we might have had the same class on Tuesdays and Thursdays and others on Mondays, Wednesdays and Fridays. It was all predictable. Almost everyone I've spoken with *ever* has had some experience of routines such as these.

With so much structure and routine, we became used to and comfortable with Ordinary robotic behaviour. It became deeply ingrained in us, so much so that when we got to college and there was less external structure, we *created* rhythms and routines for ourselves. Later, as we got out into the workplace, we continued to keep those rule-bound behaviours in place – in large part because we were afraid to do otherwise. As we were growing up, it was pounded into us: *If you don't play by the rules and meet expectations, you will fail. You won't make it to the next level. You'll fall behind. Your life will become subpar. Forever and ever.* And so we did our homework and studied for tests and showed up at school on time, fearing that we'd fail if we didn't, we wouldn't have the glorious lives promised to us. We got used to unquestioningly doing what was expected.

Again, rhythm, routine and habit aren't inherently bad. They help structure our lives and give them meaning. They calm us, allowing us to feel safe. But they also squelch creativity. They keep us from changing and growing. They make us fear unplanned deviations from the sequence; when one hits, we waste time worrying about it. Worst of all, they keep us stuck in unhealthy interpersonal patterns that hold us back and keep us from a 25th hour.

You'll remember Isabella and Matt, the colleagues in chapter 6 who were locked in conflict and struggling to get out of it. Isabella, the head of sales, was bullying Matt, who oversaw operations. Matt was miserable; he hated being yelled at for the perceived deficiencies of his team, but he didn't know what to do about it. In fact, his inner robot was helping to keep the conflict locked in place. Every time Isabella would insult him or shout at him, he responded defensively. It was a habitual action: when attacked, defend. "Oh, it wasn't me," he'd say. "Actually, you did it, not me." "I never promised that!" And on and on.

Matt eventually changed the dynamics of their relationship, using "Turn Insults into Fuel" to turn Isabella's abuse into the impetus for performance improvements on his part. But before he could do that, he needed to recognize how robotically he'd been responding and break the sequence internally. He accomplished that by using "It's My Fault" to diminish the fear he felt at not responding robotically, making the conscious decision to accept responsibility: *Yep, it's my fault. I did it. No big deal. Hey, Isabella, if you need to yell, go yell at a different robot. I'm not going to take the time to listen to you.* Before, he hadn't thought of himself as bearing responsibility. Now he did. He'd broken the sequence.

Quite often, it's not just our bosses or our organizations that keep us unhappy at work and operating inefficiently; it's our inner robot. Several years ago, a woman I know, Jane, sat down with me to talk about problems she was having at work. Among other issues, there apparently was an unwritten rule that lower-level employees couldn't leave for the day before their bosses did. Leaving before your boss did made you seem like a slacker. So after Jane and her colleagues had finished their work, they often felt compelled to sit around until six o'clock, seven o'clock, or even later, until their boss finally walked out the door. It was a huge waste of time, and it messed up their work-life balance. The time wasted was even greater since they spent hours complaining about it.

All along, Jane could have approached her boss and simply asked her, "If we're done with what we have to do, is it a big deal if we leave?" But she hadn't done that. It seemed impossible to her: the culture wouldn't allow it; it would look bad to her boss if she raised the question; her colleagues would talk about her. Listening to her, I realized that there was a deeper dynamic at play: she was afraid of doing something differently, even something as seemingly minor or insignificant as this. Like all of us, she'd developed an inner robot, and the thought of breaking with it made her deeply uncomfortable. She'd have to accept a bit of discomfort and fight her fears if she were to move ahead and save time.

Eventually, she did learn to fight her fears and break with her inner robot. She left her job and found a new one at a company whose culture aligned more closely with her values. Today, she is thriving in her career in part because of lessons she's learned from repeatedly breaking the sequence. Instead of being penalized, she often receives accolades for her Exceptional contributions.

What Your Robot Doesn't Want You to Know

Most of the time, breaking the sequence and reprogramming our inner robot will garner applause from others, helping us stand out and benefiting our careers. Have I told you about the special colourful reports I generated in my youth? Back when I was an account manager at Interep, working hard to build my career, my boss assigned me to prepare a market report that we would hand out to senior leaders. As I put it together, it occurred to me that the document was boring and hard to read. I got the idea of printing out each section of the report on a different colour paper instead of just using the usual white paper. I mean, why the hell not?

When leaders got the report, they were surprised to see a whole rainbow of colours in their hands. Not just surprised – they freaking loved it. In an organization where everyone played by the rules and did the bare minimum, that little bit of creativity blew their minds.

I don't think any of them would today remember what information that report contained, but they'd all remember that one of my first initiatives at the company was to turn in a report using multicoloured paper. I'd broken the sequence – and it got me noticed. Bear in mind, that was just one of the ways in which I was breaking the sequence back then. Another, even more important example was my determination to beat back my defensiveness and take responsibility when I felt under attack. When my boss threw me under the bus at that senior leadership meeting and I uttered the equivalent of "Oh, that was my bad," that *really* helped me stand out.

Reprogramming your robot is almost always a solid move. So don't hesitate. If you're a student in business school, what if you didn't go straight into a new job after graduation but instead took three months to work abroad? If you're a parent and you normally become frustrated with your kids when they don't do their homework, what if you tone down the criticism and offer them a special reward for getting it all done early? If you often fight with your significant other about how much they spend at the mall, what if you instead lay off and lead by example, cutting back on your own indulgences? If you're a team member and you normally attend meetings that don't seem meaningful or relevant to you, what about approaching your boss and asking if you can attend only when an agenda item is relevant for you? Whatever your circumstances and in all areas of your life, challenge yourself to completely alter your approach to the tasks before you. Not all of them, all at once. Some of them. And then, over time, more of them.

As my clients change their behaviour, they're surprised to see how much their robot was constraining them. They discover how much they can learn by adjusting their routine. And they discover how much easier it is to avoid getting sucked into the Ucks, since they're continually learning and shifting their perspectives. They find that changing things up might be a less efficient way of operating at first, costing them a small bit of time. They find, as I've suggested, that it's a bit scary. But they learn that it's worth it to take time up front to do something different and to push through their fears. Over the longer term, their productivity, confidence and happiness soar – and they move closer to that 25th hour.

Becoming Comfortable with Being Uncomfortable

To handle the fears that come with leaving behind habitual behaviour, starting small and then ramping up can help. If we were to try to change *every* habit, including some of the bigger and more significant ones, we would easily become overwhelmed. Starting with one decision or habit can give us the mojo we need to break with others. Again, look at these shifts as experiments. Maybe they'll work, maybe not. It's not a huge deal!

To reinforce that reality, make use of "What's the Worst Thing That Can Happen?", the tool for managing fear that you learned in chapter 9. When I laid off a significant portion of our workforce, I didn't have everything mapped out. It was an experiment, and there was no guarantee of success. But that was okay. What was the worst that could happen? I ran through that analysis, and the Angel on my shoulder reassured me: *You'll be fine.* Sure, I'd feel awful about unsettling the lives of the employees we'd let go. That was just something I'd have to deal with. But if the layoffs wound up hurting our business, we'd manage through it. I'd hire new people or make other operational changes to move us forward. We'd adjust and survive.

There's a second way you can deal with the fear of departing from habit: think about times in your life when you did it. We might all have robots, but none of us is *entirely* ruled by them. There are exceptions. Draw strength from those experiences. I know I do.

One of my mum's dearest and oldest friends is Beverly, a

brilliant and accomplished woman who lived across the street from us throughout my childhood and was a second mother to me (and still is). A senior administrator in our school district, Beverly inspired me and many others with her impeccable dress and general professionalism. But she also enjoyed taking a break from serious business. When we had snow days, she was the first to know that classes were cancelled and would invite my family over in our pyjamas for a scrumptious pancake breakfast. Nothing said "day off" like seeing Beverly in sweatpants and smelling those pancakes. It was such a fun way to break the sequence. Deep down, I internalized the idea that suspending a pattern could perhaps be a *good* thing. Later, when I tried to force myself to break patterns at work, remembering those days eating pancakes in my pyjamas made it easier, giving me an extra mental boost.

A third way to overcome your fears about experimentation is to become more comfortable being uncomfortable. As an exercise to make us more aware of our internal robot and help us shake it free, I challenge my clients over a period of weeks to focus on doing small things in their lives differently. If they normally brush their teeth and then shower, I want them to shower and then brush their teeth. If they typically put their right leg into their pants first and then their left leg, they are to do the opposite. If they're used to turning right when pulling out of their driveway, they are to turn left. If they're known for wearing dark suits, they are to try wearing something colourful. If they like to eat lunch at noon, they are to try eating at 1:00 pm. And so on.

This fun exercise helps you handle discomfort by teaching you that when you're plopped into the unfamiliar, you can and will figure it out. If you decide to break with your habit and go to a new coffee shop, you don't know if they'll have your favourite special coffee drink or if it will be as good there as it is at your usual place. If they don't have it, maybe you'll try another coffee drink you've never had before and find that you like it even better. If you normally go grocery shopping on Sunday night but decide to try shopping on Saturday afternoon, you might find that there's a different person behind the deli counter and you have to take more time explaining how thinly you like your turkey sliced. That's okay! Small changes like these can make us surprisingly uncomfortable. Try changing the order of the tasks in your morning routine – it's not as easy as it sounds. But we survive. And often, we find that making a tiny change feels better than we thought. We see life from new perspectives. We meet new people. We have new experiences. We come to new realizations. Change is actually very cool. And fun!

To find a 25th hour and ramp up your growth and development, make breaking the sequence the newest habit in your life. Never stop doing it. Constantly challenge yourself to break new habits – every week, every month, every day. Doing this allows you to keep things fresh, vibrant and light. You'll be uncovering and changing sterile, stubborn behaviours that aren't working for you. You'll have an easier time using other tools in this book to interact with people in new and Exceptional ways. If you're a leader, you'll model a bold, experimental approach to life for your team members, inspiring them to do it in turn.

Life doesn't have to be boring, tedious, stultifying and inefficient. Neither does work. The more comfortable you are being uncomfortable, the more you can get done, and the more fun you will have. Confront your anxieties about departing from the status quo and try something new. Laugh at your entrenched habits and the fears that hold them in place. They're ridiculous! If you struggle to break them, laugh at that, too. That silly robot. He's doing his best to hang on and hold you back. But now, with "Breaking the Sequence", you know how to beat him. So go do it!

Find Your 25th Hour: Breaking the Sequence

Let's start breaking the sequence right now. Think of an ingrained pattern that you can change, and do it. If you typically meet up with your work colleagues every morning at nine, start doing it every afternoon at three. Or do it just once a week. If your team usually meets for thirty minutes, limit it to fifteen. If you typically insert your left leg first when putting on your pants, try leading with your right. What do you notice? How do you and others adjust to the change? How does it feel? Are there any unanticipated consequences, positive or negative? If this experiment works, great. If not, make adjustments. And then go on to the next experiment.

Eleven

You're Powerful, and You Don't Even Know It!

Now that you've practised breaking a few ingrained habits, here's an important one I'd like you to tackle. Imagine it's late afternoon during a weekday and you're supposed to go out for dinner with your best friend in a few hours. You haven't picked a restaurant; the two of you agreed to make that a game-time decision. You're sitting at your desk, feeling those first small pangs of hunger, when it hits you: what you're really craving is a nice, thick piece of lasagna. And garlic bread. And some tiramisù for dessert. You know just the place – you and your friend have gone there before.

Your phone rings. It's your dinner companion asking where you'd like to meet up. How do you respond? Most of us would say something such as "Well, I'm kind of feeling like Italian tonight" or "I don't know, maybe Italian. What do you think?"

An answer like this is all too Ordinary. Damn it, you want Italian tonight. You aren't just "kind of feeling" like it. You're craving it! Yet you're backing away from expressing your true feelings. You're hedging. Maybe you don't want your friend to think you're domineering. Maybe your friend intimidates you and you tend to defer to their preferences. Whatever the case, you're not really saying what you think. You're not fully speaking your truth.

We temper or soften our communications like this all the time. I call it the "kind-of-maybe-sort-ofs". When our colleague seems peeved about an issue at work, we say something like "Yeah, maybe we should have a meeting about that" instead of "I want a meeting to discuss that" or "Let's meet this coming Tuesday to discuss it." When someone asks us for feedback about a design choice, we say, "I kind of think I might do that in blue, not green," when what we are really thinking is "That green colour is hideous. Blue is *way* better." My son Jared, who in almost every other respect is an Exceptional leader, will sometimes say, "Yeah, I think I can sort of be there at two pm" even though he knows he has something else scheduled. He doesn't want to disappoint me by telling me in no uncertain terms that he can't make it.

Or, more accurately, he's afraid to disappoint me. When we hedge or soften our communications, we're usually operating out of fear. Humans have a basic need for intimacy and relationships – we want to be liked, to fit in, to feel welcome and accepted.[1] Conversely, we have an existential dread of rubbing others the wrong way. And so we tone down what we say. We don't ask to go out for Italian when we really want to. We don't offer frank feedback about that hideous shade of green. In our minds, potentially harming a relationship feels far worse than failing to express ourselves in the moment. Add to that the fact that most of us from a very young age have witnessed people being mocked, excluded, defriended or worse because of what they said or did. We don't want that to happen to us.

Interestingly, the same robot that tells us to tone it down also intervenes on the occasions when we *do* muster the courage to speak directly. "Sure, say what you mean," our robot says, "but for heaven's sake, tack on some qualifying statements so that you don't piss anyone off or look ridiculous." And so we do. A colleague in a meeting prefaces their otherwise pointed remark with "I'm not the smartest person in the room, but . . ." or "I don't want to disrupt the flow of the conversation, but . . ." Students wondering about something in class say, "This may be a stupid question, but . . ." If someone asks us for advice or feedback, we round it out by saying "Of course, that's just my opinion."

Our habit of speaking tentatively and cautiously might seem innocuous, but it's a massive problem. Think about that colleague who is peeved about a work issue. She probably expressed her discontent in a vague way, saying something like "I'm not sure that's the ideal way to proceed, but who knows." When you in turn tell her, "Yeah, maybe we need to have a meeting about this," she could take your own equally vague or ambivalent response as a sign that you don't really hear her or care about her concerns. Since she fears coming across as rude or aggressive, she might continue to hedge, saying, "No, we don't need to – it's not really a big deal for me."

You wind up not holding the meeting, despite your nagging sense that the issue might really be bothering her. Days or weeks pass. Resentment builds on her part, and she becomes more distant and untrusting. This in turn irritates you. But you don't dare call her on it. Since neither of you has expressed yourself directly to the other, it feels weird to do so now. And so the two of you are caught in a dance of hostility and dysfunction. Before long, you're commiserating about your colleague to other team members, wasting their time. Meanwhile, the underlying issue that your colleague sort of raised never got fixed, making your team less productive. All of this continues until overt conflict breaks out between the two of you, wasting even more time and spreading bad vibes all around. You massively erode your 25th hour.

To help my clients speak more directly, I discourage them from making qualifying statements. Stop! Just don't do it! I also use a tool that I call "Be Definitive". It goes like this: throughout the day, listen to yourself speaking. When you're about to say something such as "Well, I'm kind of feeling like Italian tonight," take a second to catch yourself. Mentally label this statement Version A. Now think of how you might express yourself directly in a plainspoken way that isn't aggressive or hurtful: "I want Italian tonight." Label that Version B. When actually speaking, choose the second, more definitive way of communicating. You'll usually find that it's much shorter and more efficient.

At the end of the day, reflect on key conversations you had. Were there moments when you weren't as clear or direct as you might have been, even if you weren't aware of them in the moment? For each one, think of what a good Version B would have been. The next time you're in a similar situation, choose that way of communicating. Others will probably thank you for your clarity, since you'll often be saving them from venturing down unproductive paths or puzzling over what you mean to convey.

Version A Versus Version B

You're giving feedback to your spouse:

Version A: "Honey, that grey blouse looks fabulous, but I wonder what that yellow one you have would look like on you."

Version B: "I would definitely go with the yellow one."

You're responding negatively to an idea during a brainstorming session:

Version A: "That's an interesting thought. Sure. Let's think about that a bit more."

Version B: "I don't think that this idea will work."

You're delivering bad news about a project:

Version A: "I'm thinking we'll probably be on track to deliver the project on time, but let's see how it goes."

Version B: "We're running several weeks behind and will deliver the project a month late."

Short-Circuiting Our Power

Getting into the habit of communicating more directly can help you enjoy healthier relationships and move toward a 25th hour, but there's deeper work to be done. If you often operate in "kind-of-maybe-sort-of" mode, you're hobbled by a more basic and far-reaching problem: you're alienated from your own power.

Most of us have little idea of how powerful we are. I'm not talking about the influence we have by virtue of our job titles; I'm talking about our superpowers as people – our ability to be analytical, say, or our ability to listen and empathize or our ability to penetrate to the core of an idea. When we're in touch with our own power, we *own* who we are and what we're about. We use our superpowers to the fullest, projecting our will into the world through our words and actions – without all the ambiguity and qualifiers. Setting aside our fears, we move through the world with confidence and poise. We take risks to achieve our goals and live with integrity.

Conversely, when we're out of touch with our own power, we remain prisoners to our fears and prevent ourselves from projecting our personalities out into the world. We fall into unhelpful patterns of blaming others and then developing cases of the Ucks. We limit ourselves, telling ourselves that we're not capable of tackling certain challenges, which gives us an excuse to behave timidly and reactively and pass up opportunities. We waste large amounts of time and hold back our career progress. Ultimately, we become stuck, and our lives feel unsatisfying and frustrating. Our Devil has eroded our power.

If you're like most people, the very idea that you might be powerful gives you the jitters. When I ask my clients if they're powerful, they almost always don't know how to respond. They become fidgety. They stay silent. This is true even of people who are narcissistic or egotistical. Although power can seem glamorous, it also has a negative connotation for most of us, especially in a corporate context, just as words such as "fault" or "blame" do. We speak of people disparagingly as being power hungry or power grubbing. We think of such people as being egotistical, narcissistic or unfeeling. That's the *last* way we want to come across, either to others or to ourselves. So when someone asks us whether we're powerful, we feel awkward.

When others compliment you for a special strength or accomplishment, do you respond gracefully and directly by saying a simple "Thanks"? Or do you instinctively diminish your power by attempting to project modesty, whether by crediting others around you, claiming that your strength or accomplishment is no big deal, or instantly returning the compliment?

Because we're so awkward around our own power, we wind up lying to ourselves and others. I'm not talking about literal lying, such as cheating or deceiving in the usual sense. I mean that we fail to own up to who we really are, including both our weaknesses and the unique gifts we've been given. The first homework assignment I give new clients is to list twenty-five strengths and weaknesses about themselves. Every client who walks through my door – every one, from top-tier CEOs to students – has a distorted and false sense of their own capacities. They list weaknesses that they obviously don't have. And they fail to register their obvious strengths. Since they're unintentionally lying to themselves, they systematically undercut their power in their own minds and fail to project it into the world.

Their lack of confidence causes them to waste time overpreparing when they don't need to. It also causes them to make decisions and organize their lives in ways that not only are wasteful but leave them unhappy and stressed out.

Maggie, the doctor of physical therapy whom I mentioned briefly in chapter 1, is a good example. As a patient of hers, I found her to be extremely skilled – in fact, the best practitioner I've encountered. Yet I also saw that she was lying to herself and had no sense of her own power. As a self-professed people pleaser by temperament, she had developed a nasty habit of diminishing herself in her own mind to keep others happy. She was constantly qualifying the value she brought to her practice. When a client asked what she charged for her sessions, she would tell them but then tack on something such as, "Oh, but I'm not really worth all that much." When she told me about patients she had helped, she instantly downplayed her contribution by saying, "Well, that didn't really have anything to do with me. The effort *they* put into their treatment made all the difference." As she remembered, "I never owned my role in anybody's experience. I would qualify myself and make myself really small to feel worthy of people coming in to see me."

Those habits were bad enough, but Maggie's inability to understand and own her superpowers also led her to run her life in ways that eroded her happiness. Uncertain about her value and eager for her clients to like her, she systematically undercharged them and even worked extra hours without pay. A session that was scheduled for thirty minutes would somehow turn into ninety. Maggie was delighted to be of service, but she was too afraid to ask for a supplemental fee. She also found herself working longer hours than she wanted to because she was afraid to say no to clients who sought her services. She was equally fearful outside the office. Would she run her daughter's Girl Scout troop? Absolutely. Would she run errands for her mother? Of course. Would she do a favour for an aunt? You bet. Although she needed to take time for herself, her Devil told her to sacrifice it so that she wouldn't disappoint others.

Over time, the accumulation of fear-based decisions left her feeling burned out and negative. "The best way I can describe it," she said, is that "[I was] constantly resenting my work. Something that I used to love, I just started to resent it because I felt so undervalued, which of course came from me. I was just constantly proving my own worth in my mind." At home, she was exhausted and overwhelmed. When I asked her if she might take an hour out of her day to take care of her own health, she told me that she didn't even know how she would manage it. Not only did she not have a 25th hour; to her, it felt as though she had only twenty hours in a day or even less.

Bear in mind, Maggie is accomplished – she has a doctorate degree, for heaven's sake – yet still she felt an abiding sense of powerlessness. That's hardly unusual. I've found that even the wealthiest, most successful, most authoritative people are often secretly unhappy because they're tragically detached from their own power.

Take Brendon, another client of mine. As the founder and CEO of an investment firm, he had built great wealth because of his uncanny ability to pick winning stocks in which to invest. Outwardly, he seemed confident and fulfilled, but the truth was much different. When he came to me several years ago, he told me that he wanted me to "teach him" how to be a CEO – a request that reflected nothing more than his innate fears and lack of confidence. As I discovered, he was so fearful that he felt intimidated by his industry peers. One gentleman in particular, Tony, really had his number. As a frequent guest on industry panels, Tony had more presence than Brendon. Although that might just have reflected Tony's confidence and swagger, Brendon interpreted it as a sign that he, Brendon, was distinctly "less than" – less intelligent, likable and charismatic than Tony. That bugged Brendon and caused him to waste time trying to befriend Tony, conduct business with him and gain his validation.

Brendon's disconnection from his own power was also degrading his decision-making. Bill, a junior partner at Brendon's firm, was demanding that Brendon give him an equal decision-making stake. Although Brendon knew that Bill wasn't senior leader material, he was ready to agree to give Bill what he wanted. Why? Because he was petrified that if he said no, Bill would leave the firm and go to work for a competitor. Brendon's firm was doing well, and he didn't want to rock the boat. In fact, Bill would have made a terrible manager for a whole slew of reasons. It never occurred to Brendon that he had superpowers of his own as a leader and could run his company successfully with or without Bill. He also didn't recognize that by giving Bill more authority, he risked diluting his own leadership, a move that could have grave consequences for the firm.

Getting in Touch with Your Power

I was able to save Brendon from making that terrible move and help him get over his inferiority complex with Tony. I also managed to help Maggie understand and accept her real power. In each of those cases, I had just the right tool in my toolbox, a strategy I'd invented years earlier to help myself build up my own mojo. Yes, the coach's coach has also struggled mightily with a lack of confidence!

As I mentioned in chapter 1, I used to think of myself as uncreative and unimaginative, which unbeknownst to me was a big drag on my career. That ended about a decade ago, when a client called bullshit on me and helped me understand that my supposed lack of creativity was just my Devil talking. In truth, I was highly creative – not in some conventional arts-and-crafts sense but in how I thought about problems and communicated with others. Suddenly, I understood my own power as never before. I clearly lacked skill in many areas, but I knew right then that I was a great teacher and coach, precisely because I was applying creativity. Creativity was my superpower, one that was already enabling me to help people and change their lives.

I'll never forget: a few minutes after that pivotal conversation, as I stepped into an elevator on the way out of the building, I had another epiphany. I happened to be alone, but not really: the elevator was mirrored, so I was staring at my image from multiple angles. I don't know what possessed me to do this, but as the elevator descended, I stared at my image and said out loud, "You, Neal, are powerful. You are one powerful dude in being able to use your creativity to help this many people over so many years. That's your superpower."

Research has suggested that positive affirmations can bring us all kinds of benefits, including by helping us build our self-esteem.[2] That was true for me. Something about stating those words out loud while staring at myself eyeball to eyeball made a profound impression. When I left the building that day, I felt more empowered as a coach and teacher. I was more excited and eager to project my own unique personality in my work by creating new tools. In the months and years afterward, my output of new tools went through the roof. I became more productive in everything I did because I could use my power in more directed ways. I stopped lying to myself, convincing myself that I couldn't do certain tasks and making excuses for not even trying – and instead started taking more risks.

I've since given this exercise a name: "I Am Powerful". I invite you to try it. Look into a mirror and, addressing yourself by your first name, tell yourself that you're powerful. If you can, be more specific. Tell yourself *why* you're powerful: "I'm an incredible communicator who knows how to inspire my colleagues," "I'm a salesperson who not only drives revenue but uses my natural empathy to truly help my customers," or "I'm not only great at calculus, I'm a strong and flexible learner who can master any concept that a professor in any of my subjects throws at me." You get the idea. Identify your superpower. Or more than one of them. Feel free to go into even greater detail: "Last semester, when I took advanced calculus, I struggled at first, but I studied every night and by the time of the final exam, I knew it cold. I rule when it comes to puzzling out and unpacking abstract ideas."

Does affirming your power to yourself like this feel a little odd at first? Yes! But I can tell you, it works. As Maggie recalled, running through "I Am Powerful" "was awful in the beginning. Sometimes I couldn't even get the words out. It was just so unfamiliar. For a person who was so used to playing small, for me to look at my reflection and be like 'You're exceptionally good at what you do' – that felt indulgent. It felt powerful and scary. Like, who was I to say that to myself?" She was so uncomfortable that she sometimes couldn't even get the words out. She came up with a workaround: she wrote the words on a Post-it note and stuck it onto the mirror. That's something you might try if you find yourself struggling.

Maggie's persistence with this tool paid off. As the weeks passed, she found it easier to tell herself the truth about her own power. Today, she can do it without any trouble; she's deeply internalized her self-worth. The broader impacts on her life have been remarkable: she had the courage to raise her prices significantly across the board – not out of greed but to better reflect the value she knows she brings to her clients. She also stopped always saying yes to her clients, a decision that has created time in her week to engage in creative pursuits that give her joy. "Everything became so intentional," she remarked. "I began intentionally caring for myself in a different way, which has made me an exceedingly better practitioner." Rather than feeling exhausted and burned out, she now feels alive, energized and better able to show up as her best self both at work and at home.

With Brendon, I used "I Am Powerful" alongside other tools to help him not only feel more confident and aware of his power but redirect his decision-making. By using "What's the Intent?", for example, he was able to see that what Bill really wanted wasn't equal power but better financial compensation. Brendon created a plan to give that to Bill *without* making Bill a managing partner and diminishing his own authority. In devising and implementing that solution, he learned that he could project his power by saying no when he needed to, and it wouldn't cause everything to blow up. His fears subsided, as did the time he wasted spiralling over them.

To further help Brendon with his feelings of insecurity, I had him spend more time with Tony and get to know him as a person. As Brendon discovered, Tony didn't move on some elevated plane. Behind the facade, he had the same self-doubts that Brendon did. When Brendon really analysed it, he was just as strong and valuable a leader in their industry as Tony was. Before long, he began to project his own power more, seeing himself and behaving like a senior figure or, as we call it, a statesman. Now *Brendon* was the one stepping out and serving in public on industry panels. He had realized the truth: he was very powerful, and he hadn't even known it. Before long, others started to realize it, too. While previously Brendon had envied Tony and tried to befriend him and approach him for opportunities, now Tony is the one chasing Brendon. Who would have thought?

Remembering Your Power

I don't mean to suggest that Maggie and Brendon fully grasped their power all at once thanks to "I Am Powerful". Their journey toward confidence and a more authentic and fulfilling way of living remains ongoing, as does my own. Even as we've learned to understand our own unique strengths and mobilize them without fear, we still backslide. New situations arise that trigger our old fears, awakening our Devil, who in turn starts yapping in our ears and prompting us to revert to our old habits. But there's an important difference. In "I Am Powerful", we now have a tool that we can use to manage ourselves in such moments and get back on track.

After Maggie started using "I Am Powerful", she went through a difficult period of conflict with various family members. To calm down and remind herself of her own power, she began glancing at herself in the rearview mirror while driving and saying, "I've got me," or "You've got this." During one especially heated conversation, she hit the pause button, excused herself and went to the bathroom. Looking in the mirror, she repeated to herself, "I've got this." It wasn't the classic form of "I Am Powerful", in which we explicitly identify our superpower for ourselves. Rather, she was using a kind of shorthand, reminding herself that she was powerful enough in a general sense to persevere through the situation. Her self-affirmation worked; she was able to stay calm and behave in an Exceptional way, even when her Devil tried to get her to run wild. With any of my tools, there's no need to be a purist. Once you learn the basics of managing yourself, you can make tweaks that you find helpful.

On another occasion, Maggie found that words alone weren't enough, so I prompted her to enhance "I Am Powerful". To fully project her power, she would have to confront a longtime client of hers and let them know that she was raising her rates. She knew that client would push back aggressively, putting Maggie in the position of either caving in or having to fire the client. The mere prospect of firing a client triggered her old fears about not being good enough, and she didn't know if she could go through with it. To bolster her and help her take difficult action, I asked her to name the most empowered woman that she could think of. Her answer: the action character Wonder Woman. I asked her to schedule a conversation with her client. Before she went into the conversation, she was to imagine Wonder Woman standing before her, and she was to imagine *herself* as Wonder Woman. She did that, and it gave her that extra bit of confidence and courage she needed to make the right move for herself. She wound up firing her client. Although it was difficult, she looks back on it as one of the most important decisions she made to set her career on a better track.

We began this chapter by breaking some bad habits, but as I hope you now see, it's equally important to cultivate new, healthier ones. Reminding yourself of your own power and operating from a place of truth is a great place to start. I don't care when or where you do it – whether in an elevator or your bathroom mirror at home, whether first thing in the morning or as you're glancing at the rearview mirror during your commute. I just care that you're consistent and clear in articulating the uncomfortable but energizing truth about yourself and that you look yourself in the eye as you do it.

The world is quick to tell us why we're wrong, incompetent, worthless or less than. We've grown up programming our robots to feel uncertain about standing tall and owning who we really are. You can break free of that and change your life in the process. You can add to the quantity of your time and improve its quality, making your life feel more expansive. You can wield your superpowers more deliberately to influence others, solve problems and help them succeed. You can take your own growth much further. All it takes is three simple words, repeated over and over, until you believe it deep down: "I am powerful."

Find Your 25th Hour: I Am Powerful

This exercise is for leaders, but anyone can adapt it to fit their own role in life. Get out a paper and pen and set a timer for ten minutes. Write out an answer to the question "Am I a good leader?" Look at your answer and the language you used. In making positive statements about yourself, did you hem and haw, adding qualifiers? Did you answer in an abstract, oblique or confusing way? That's Version A. Now write a clear, concise, direct statement about how and why you're a good leader (or parent or teacher or attorney or whatever you happen to be). That's Version B. Post this version in a place where you'll see it often. Keep it alive in your mind to remind yourself that you, too, are uniquely gifted and powerful.

Twelve

Give Yourself the Gift of Cookies

Not long ago, my daughter-in-law Gabrielle found herself veering off track in her quest for a 25th hour. She was finishing graduate school to become a physician's assistant, and although she'd mastered her coursework, she began to spiral as her last set of final exams approached. Her Devil was whispering into her ear such unhelpful messages as "You're going to fail. You'll have to repeat this year's coursework. It will totally suck. Nobody will want to hire you. You'll have to take some crappy job rather than the one you want. Maybe you won't even get a job!"

I can assure you that those thoughts were unfounded. Gabrielle is brilliant – and I'm not just saying that because she married my son. Since grade school, she's distinguished herself academically, earning straight A's and winning awards. I'm not sure she's ever *not* got an A. Yet with finals and a job search looming, she became frazzled and couldn't see any of that. Her Angel fell asleep on the job, while her Devil was sucking down the Red Bulls and working overtime.

Gabrielle needed to manage herself through those difficult weeks by applying a number of strategies, including one I discussed in chapter 9, "What's the Worst Thing That Can Happen?". In her case, the worst thing that could happen was that, yes, she'd have to repeat some classes and graduate late. The chance of that, when we considered it objectively, was zero. An invasion of talking squirrels was more likely than her bombing her exams. Why was she worrying so much about something that was certain not to happen?

Breaking down Gabrielle's situation in this rational way would tamp down her Devil. But instead of just neutralizing negativity in her mind, why not also inject a bit of positivity? One way of doing that would be to use the "I Am Powerful" tool described in chapter 11. But there was another technique that I thought would help Gabrielle, one that was both fun to use and nicely sweet: Gabrielle could give herself a cookie.

Most people think of cookies as a delicious treat. I do, too – a delicious *emotional and mental* treat that we can use to handle ourselves better. My "Cookies" tool, as I call it, is the paying of a compliment or the offering of favourable feedback. We all need emotional cookies during the workday, especially when we're under stress. We need to hear "You did a great job on that project," "The report was really good," "I loved how you handled that negotiation." Even the A grade on a term paper is a cookie. So is a comment from our spouse that we're good-looking and they're so happy to be by our side, or one from our neighbours that our lawn looks amazing and they just love seeing it out their kitchen window.

You might wonder why I call compliments cookies instead of, say, brownies, doughnuts or slices of Key lime pie. I'm sorry, but it really does have to be cookies. When I was a kid, I sometimes found myself craving something sweet during the late afternoons as dinner was approaching. But eating a sweet was a big no-no in our house; my mother allowed us dessert only *after* dinner. Yet my sister and I didn't adhere slavishly to the rules; sometimes she would sneak me one of my favourite cookies before dinner. I can't describe the euphoria I felt at beating the system; it was as if I'd won the lottery. As I wiped the crumbs from my mouth and gulped down a cup of milk, I had so much positive energy. I was just *happy*.

Unfortunately, those of us stuck in an Ordinary mindset rely on others in our lives to give us the emotional cookies we need to stay happy and balanced. Sometimes we crave positive affirmation so much that we try to squeeze it out of other people. We show up at our boss's office and have a conversation with the real purpose not of solving a problem or building a healthy, trusting relationship but simply trying to extract cookies. We fish for compliments from our friends or family members and hand out cookies to them for the sole purpose of getting some back in return. Despite our best efforts, we *still* don't get the cookies we need. We might not find compliments we receive that satisfying. Sure, our boss might have complimented us for handling one project, but why didn't they give us credit for tackling a second one? In the absence of consistent, positive feedback, we wonder how we're doing, and our insecurities crop up. As we become more cookie starved, we wind up like Gabrielle, vulnerable to our Devil and to wasting time on anxious spiralling.

A big part of positioning ourselves for long-term growth and development is learning to recognize our emotional hunger and give *ourselves* cookies. At first glance, the idea of paying yourself a compliment might seem odd. Aren't we being needy in requiring so much affirmation or egotistical or self-absorbed in telling ourselves how great we are? Absolutely not. We're being human. Even the most confident among us need validation, just as we need caloric intake to keep our bodies running.[1] We need to know that we're on the right track and making progress toward our goals. And as adults, we need to provide that validation for *ourselves*, just as we provide ourselves with food, clothing and other necessities. We can't presume that someone else is going to stick a gold star on our homework, as our teachers did in elementary school. It's up to *us* to manage ourselves this way.

How to Give a Cookie

The "Cookies" technique resembles "I Am Powerful". Look at yourself in a mirror and pay yourself a compliment out loud. Make it meaningful, something such as "I'm a fantastic student. I crushed that last test" or "I was incredible back there helping out my colleague with her problem" or "The way I ran that board meeting was top notch. It was not merely productive but also enjoyable for everyone at the table." Taking your cue from "Gratitude Equals Joy", you can formulate these compliments, if you wish, as expressions of thankfulness: "Thanks for being such a great student and crushing that test." "Thanks for being such a great colleague." "Thanks for being the best leader this company has ever had."

Cookies are super fun, and they really do work. Gabrielle could tell herself, "Thanks for being such a hard worker," "Thanks for being so attentive in class," "Thanks for being such a quick study when it comes to absorbing new concepts." Such small bursts of self-affirmation redirect the Devil, allowing us to focus on facts rather than a negative narrative. Unsurprisingly, she crushed her finals and graduated with honours. Today, she is thriving in her career.

The use of self-affirmation in a challenging situation is what we might call Cookies 101. There's an advanced technique, which is to give yourself cookies on a regular basis, *before* your Devil has a chance to grab hold of you. I recommend doing so once a day or even more frequently. Of course, if you were to eat that many actual cookies, you would soon find yourself growing out of your clothes. Emotional cookies are different. I'm not sure that you can give yourself too many of them.

If you work in an office, give yourself a cookie during your morning commute or while taking a bathroom break between meetings. I conduct most of my coaching sessions on Zoom. When a session ends and before I turn the camera on my computer off, I'll find myself staring at my own image for a moment. I'll take the opportunity to munch on a cookie. "Neal," I'll say, "you rocked it in that session. You did such a good job tracking the issue, and you quickly spotted what was going on beneath the surface." Or "Neal, you did a great job of calming John down and then redirecting him to regain focus. That will absolutely help him. Nice work!" If I feel hungrier on a given day, I'll go into more detail. "What you did amazingly well today was utilization of time and the examples that you used. You showed professional vulnerability, and you introduced the two most important tools in thirty minutes. I don't remember you ever doing that quite as efficiently before. Nice job."

Again, I'm not being egotistical; I'm saying these things to myself, not other people. And I'm doing it for a reason: by noting something positive about myself or remarking on a recent achievement, I become more energized and confident. With my doubts and insecurities at bay, I can show up more fully as myself, breaking free of my Devil and behaving in ways that are Exceptional.

Like "I Am Powerful", "Cookies" will feel wildly uncomfortable at first as we struggle with the fear that we're being disagreeably boastful or immodest. If we harbour a perfectionist complex, we might feel that we don't deserve compliments. We presume that there's some ideal out there that we must attain, and we feel reluctant to affirm ourselves because we're painfully aware that we haven't reached it. I hate to break it to you: perfection doesn't exist. You might think that chocolate is the absolute perfect flavour of ice cream, but rest assured, there's someone else out there who likes strawberry better. So stop presuming that you need to be chocolate. And toss out the idea that you don't deserve cookies. A productive life wouldn't be possible without the emotional fuel that cookies give us. It certainly wouldn't be as sweet.

Cookies for All

Although an appreciation of cookies is vital for everyone, it becomes even more important as we progress in our careers and take on leadership roles. Since leaders are charged with motivating team members, they must make a habit of dispensing cookies freely to team members. Unfortunately, most leaders I've seen are way too stingy with both cookies and feedback in general. That's not surprising, since research suggests that most of us tend to underestimate how meaningful compliments are to others.[2]

When leaders do tell team members how they're doing, they tend to emphasize constructive criticism (and sometimes the destructive variety) rather than celebrating team members' strengths or accomplishments. They forget how meaningful compliments are when they come from a boss and how much positive reinforcement does to keep their team members' Devils at bay. They also forget that in the absence of cookies, team members can feel underappreciated at work, and their motivation can diminish.

If you lead or manage others, how often do you hand out cookies? Do entire days go by without your dispensing one? If so, you've got work to do. Think about who you hand them out to and under what circumstances. Do you give them only to your favourites on the team, or do you spread them out widely? Do you hand them out only during certain kinds of encounters, such as formal meetings and performance reviews? Do you wait for team members to prod you into paying them compliments? It might be hard for you to judge your own behaviour accurately, so I recommend asking others around you what they observe. Perhaps you're offering enough positive reinforcement, but then again, perhaps not.

In chapter 7, I told you about Marcus, the young company president who had a tough relationship with his father and was able to make progress by learning to express more gratitude. It might not surprise you to learn that Marcus was terrible at handing out cookies. It's a common pattern; if we're not attuned to feeling gratitude toward others, we often won't think of paying them compliments. When I first met Marcus, he hardly ever handed out cookies. It just never occurred to him to do so, and he also believed – quite incorrectly – that saying nice things to people would make him come across as a soft leader. As a result, others around him were starved for cookies, and he had no clue.

I gave Marcus a homework assignment: he wasn't simply to start handing out cookies; he was to go *crazy*, becoming a full-blown cookie monster. That felt strange to him, but he decided to go with it. One of the first people to whom he offered a cookie was an hourly employee named Ralph who performed maintenance work at a company-owned facility. He went up to Ralph one day as he worked and said, "Hey, I really appreciate you cleaning up. You're doing a great job with that. The floor looks much better."

Ralph stopped what he was doing and spent several minutes telling him how much it meant to him that Marcus had complimented him. "I can't believe you're saying this to me right now," he said. "I can't tell you how meaningful that is. I'm constantly cleaning up and taking care of people, and I often do it after hours when nobody's around. Nobody ever acknowledges the work I do or tells me I'm doing a good job. They just take it for granted. The most I'll get is a nod or a hello, but even that's pretty rare." As Marcus later learned, Ralph was so blown away that he texted his wife and kids immediately after Marcus left and told them what a great day he was having. When they asked him why, he told them that the president of the company had approached him to pay him a compliment and express his thanks.

This exercise of becoming a cookie monster (which, by the way, I would suggest for all leaders) really stuck with Marcus. He now understands the great power we have thanks to the humble cookie.

Whenever we do a coaching session, he makes sure to thank me for my contribution. And he does the same with his team members, fuelling their happiness on the job and motivation to perform.

Like expressions of gratitude, paying compliments serves to create positive contagion. When team members receive meaningful compliments, especially from a boss, a supervisor or someone else they respect, they see the world in a more positive light and become more likely to hand out cookies to others. They also tell others in their lives about the cookie they received, improving their mood and making them more likely to hand out compliments, too. As I've seen, an entire meeting can perk up when those present observe someone smiling and then find out that her boss's boss paid her a compliment. Leaders who give compliments also model this prosocial behaviour. Over time, others on the team will pay more compliments, which can help improve productivity. Researchers have found that people on high-performing teams pay significantly more compliments to one another relative to how many criticisms they dole out than people on lower-performing teams do.[3]

To get the most bang for your cookie buck, make sure you're giving cookies to others swiftly, directly and with an appropriate level of detail. If you leave out the specifics, your compliment can come across as generic and inauthentic. But there's no need to ramble on, as that can seem forced or weird. "Hey, Frank," you might say, "that piece that you wrote was exceptional because I understood it quickly, it was concise and it had the impact for the mission. Thank you." That's three cookies in one simple statement. Clear and to the point. No time wasted on a lengthy monologue. Then you pause and wait for a response, preparing yourself for a bit of awkwardness. Your team members might feel just as strange receiving compliments as you would. But they'll definitely appreciate it.

Tasty and Less Tasty Cookies: Some Examples

Tasty Cookies . . .

"Great job tying the content to the plan!"

"I noticed that you're truly stepping it up based on the feedback you received last week. Nice!"

"The extra effort that you're showing is really paying off. So many people are commenting and appreciating your efforts."

"Well done on that extra project and assignment. I really appreciate your focus and efforts to go above and beyond."

Less Tasty Cookies . . .

"Keep up the good work." (too vague, almost meaningless)

"About time this came together." (an insult disguised as a compliment)

"I knew you had it in you." (puts the focus on you, not them)

"Thanks for trying. Maybe next time." (again, vague; talks about their effort rather than their actual performance)

Damn, You're Good

As leaders start handing out more cookies to others, they must save some for themselves. In fact, I would argue that the most important cookies for leaders are the ones they give themselves. You see, leaders tend to be uniquely cookie starved. And the further you proceed in your career and the higher you go in an organization, the more cookie starved you become. Fewer people think to tell you what a great job you're doing or offer you any kind of feedback. The CEO *hardly ever* receives compliments. It's not as though a busy board member is going to call up a CEO and say, "I just want you to know, I love the way you're running those town hall meetings with the company." A veteran executive's junior colleagues also aren't likely to offer cookies very often; they're looking to their leader to dole them out to *them*. Even when people do pay compliments to CEOs and other senior leaders, they don't usually land the way Marcus's cookie did with Ralph. Instead, leaders brush them off, wondering whether a more junior colleague might be trying to ingratiate themselves with them or obtain some kind of favour.

It's no fun trying to run a team or organization when you operate in a cookie-free zone. I told you earlier how I fell into a period of crisis and doubt while serving as the CEO of Triton and had to use "Fire Yourself" and "What's the Worst Thing That Can Happen?" to pull myself out. That was truly one of the top two or three worst professional crises of my life and it sent me into the granddaddy of all mental swirls. A big part of it, as I've conveyed, had to do with the lack of feedback from others. I was under financial pressure and I had the same impostor syndrome that many relatively inexperienced leaders feel. It was unclear to me and hard for me to know if I was doing a good job or not.

Somehow I got the idea of mobilizing the power of cookies to help me through. I'd been handing out cookies to my team and clients in my coaching, and I'd been teaching them to pay their team members compliments as a way of fuelling their motivation and improving their productivity. Now I realized how important it was for me as a leader to pay compliments to myself.

In addition to the "Cookie" tool, which acknowledged a specific accomplishment of mine, I devised a slightly different version called

"I'm Really Good at What I Do" that served as a general affirmation of my talents or abilities. I started a daily practice of looking in the mirror and acknowledging my growth and contributions, including when I excelled at a task. I told myself, "You're really good at what you do. You have made it to this point and you'll prevail again. You'll figure it out. You can do it. You can grasp the opportunity in front of you."

I encourage you to adopt "You're Really Good at What You Do" as well. If nothing else, it's an exercise in truth telling. Certainly you wouldn't have progressed so far in your career were you not amazing at what you do. Remind yourself of that – each and every day. I did back then, and my fears subsided. My energy and confidence returned. People around me noticed. They said that there was "something different" about me, although they couldn't quite place what it was. You know what it was? I had stopped the negative contagion that my unchecked fears had been feeding and instead started a dynamic of positive contagion.

Yet another variant of the cookie that leaders can practise is something I call "I Did This". One client of mine, Ellen, cofounded a startup with three other partners. The firm grew fast, and today it's worth nearly a billion dollars – a massive accomplishment. Of the founding partners, Ellen has played the greatest role in the company's success. Yet amid her fear and doubt, she forgets to credit her own efforts. This is a common trap. Because leaders oversee teams of people, they're used to crediting others and neglect to acknowledge the role that they themselves play.

It can be so powerful to look yourself in the mirror on a frequent basis and say, "Yep, I did this." You're not doing this in a narcissistic or egotistical way. You're not saying that *only* you did this. You're just taking a moment to credit your own efforts, proceeding on the baseline assumption that of course it was a team effort. Reminding yourself that *you* led your team or organization's success allows you to consider your success in a more rational, balanced way that fuels your self-confidence. It's a great way to counter impostor syndrome so that you can boldly attack the challenges before you.

Whether you're a leader or just starting out in your career, pay more attention to cookies than you currently do. It takes only a few seconds to offer yourself or others a sweet treat, there is no financial cost to you and the benefits are enormous. All of us need regular boosts to our self-confidence. And all of us are equipped to deliver them. So start practising. Starting today, tell someone how great they are. Tell yourself, too. You'll be happier for it. By reducing those devilish voices of fear and insecurity in your head, you'll support your ongoing growth and add to your 25th hour.

Find Your 25th Hour: Cookies

Do you feel a case of the Ucks coming on? Here's an idea for you: hand out some cookies to others around you. Pretend it's the holidays and think of yourself as Santa Claus or Hanukkah Harry. Set a goal for yourself: to pay ten compliments a day for the next three days. Heck, make it fifteen. You'll come away feeling *great* and enhancing your relationships with others. It's fun to receive cookies, but it's also pretty amazing to hand them out. You'll be able to go home at the end of the day and say, "I've made the lives of all those people a little bit better." Just think of the positive contagion you'll spread.

Thirteen

Are You Mediocre?

I have a confession to make, one that I'm sure you'll find shocking. I'm mediocre. Not good or even decent. Mediocre. All of us are at times, some of us more frequently. And all of us have it in us *not* to be. Let me explain by way of a story.

Back in 2015, when my team and I were preparing to sell Triton, I devised a plan for operating our business in the years to come that I knew would add significant value. I mean, the plan was rock solid. It was freaking awesome. It would send productivity through the roof. All we needed to do was execute on it, the sooner, the better.

I could have put my plan into place immediately. I was the CEO, after all. But I didn't. Instead, I waited. For months. And then more months. Eventually a private equity firm bought us – they thought the plan was awesome, too. Two weeks after the sale went through, I began executing the plan.

Why did I wait so long? I could string together a vague, long-winded explanation for you, something about optimal market conditions or client initiatives. The truth was that I wimped out. I was mediocre.

You see, the plan called for us to restructure the company and lay people off (an episode I referred to in a previous chapter). That was scary and uncomfortable for me; I feared that the layoffs would lower morale among our remaining workers. Also, I didn't know for sure that the plan would work. What if it didn't? By waiting until after we sold, I'd be able to paint the plan as our new owner's doing. The layoffs, I'd imply, were the private equity firm's fault. *It* was the bad guy, not me. And if the plan didn't work, it, not I, would be left looking dumb.

Mediocre.

Let me clarify. When people use "mediocre" in a professional context, they often refer to raw performance and a lack of competence. A mediocre salesperson lands twenty deals a year, while a good one lands thirty, an excellent one forty. I think of mediocrity differently – not just as weak performance or incompetence but as *cowardice*.

Mediocrity is Ordinary behaviour through and through. It's taking the easy way out when you could have taken the harder, more fulfilling one. It's sticking to what's safe or comfortable. It's covering your ass. It's shrinking from having the hard conversations. It's refraining from raising your hand in a meeting and saying what you *really* think. It's staying quiet about a problem you discover rather than telling people about it. It's thinking of a great idea and then not sharing it for fear of looking ridiculous.

Behaving in mediocre ways erodes performance and impedes our growth, not least because it wastes time. When we fail to speak up, we let problems fester, to the point where we or others must spend much more time unravelling them later. When we avoid hard conversations with others, we waste unnecessary time perseverating about the issues at hand. When we put off tough decisions, we waste time that we could have spent moving our teams and organizations forward. My failure to implement our strategic plan in a timely way cost our company a whole year! It also ate into my personal 25th hour. During that time, I had to sustain the internal tension of not doing what I knew deep down I had to do. That entailed many hours spent worrying about the future and feeling misgivings about our present situation.

I'd like you to do something: take out a blank sheet of paper and draw a horizontal line through the middle. Draw one dot just below that line and another one just above it. Draw a third dot way above the line, near the top of the sheet. This line is what I call the "Line of Mediocrity". If you're just below the line, you're thoroughly mediocre. If you're just above it, you're what most people would consider "good" in your job but still largely mediocre. And if you're way above, you're an Exceptional employee or leader.

What Kind of Professional Are *You*?

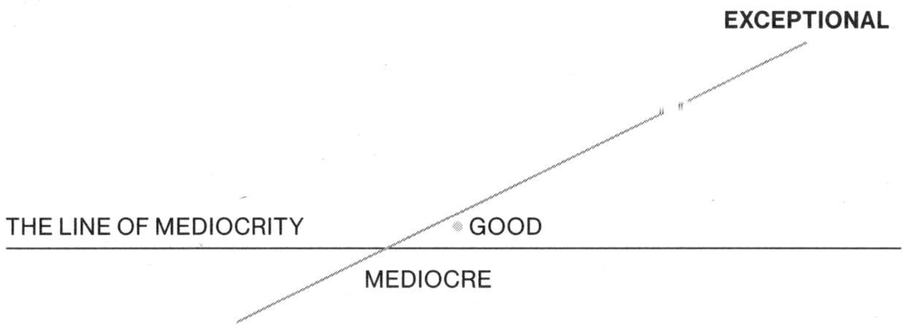

I would contend that almost everyone in an organization resides closely on either side of the Line of Mediocrity. Those of us who are just below it put out performance that isn't terrible but merely average. The reason, by and large, is that we're content to go with the flow and do the minimum required of us. We're likeable and competent enough that we probably won't get fired. But we phone it in. We don't take risks. We don't try to improve. We don't take the initiative. We don't think of creative solutions. We don't put in extra effort unless we know our boss is watching.

Most of us are better than this, but not by much. We're just slightly above the line of mediocrity. Yes, we do a good job compared with those below the line. We shine at times and get promoted, and our bosses identify us as solid performers. But we likewise usually fail to show courage and take risks. Maybe, on occasion, we'll stick our neck out in a meeting, but most of the time we hedge and waffle rather than taking a risk and speaking decisively. Unlike those below the line, we care enough to have creative ideas, but not enough to tell others about them. If we spot a problem at work that needs addressing, we'll try to alert someone, but we'll do it in a way that covers our own butt.

Then there are those precious few employees and leaders at the very top of the chart, way above the line of mediocrity. You know who these people are within teams and organizations – they stand out for their willingness to make themselves uncomfortable when necessary. They make the tough decisions, knowing that they might have to defend their position. They speak up definitively, even if there's some risk of blowback, because they know it's the right thing to do. They share their ideas, not because they think they're always correct but because they stand by the courage of their convictions.

If you're honest with yourself, where do you reside relative to the line of mediocrity? And if you're not way above the line, what the heck are you going to do about it?

Yes, It *Is* Your Job

In my work with clients, I find that there's a story people often tell that underlies and reinforces a lot of mediocre behaviour. It's the comforting idea that *it's not my job*. You're walking in the park and you come upon a piece of trash. There happens to be a trash can nearby. Do you pick up the trash? Most of us don't, reasoning that it's not *our* job to do that. The town government that runs the park pays people to do that. Why waste our time on it?

The notion that we have very circumscribed roles or "jobs" and that we aren't obliged to veer outside them is deeply embedded. We've been thinking this way since our grade-school teachers asked us to clean up a mess and we said, "But I didn't do it!" As adults, most of us robotically perpetuate "it's not my job" thinking in the workplace, where it becomes a ready excuse for cowardice and mediocrity. How often do you hear someone say that a task is "above my pay grade"? Mediocre!

We might be on the sales team and attend a meeting with colleagues from marketing. An intriguing but risky idea about the company's new marketing campaign occurs to us, but we choose not to share it, telling ourselves, "Well, I'm not on the marketing team, so it's not my job to have creative ideas in that area." Our idea might have had some merit, spurring others to refine it and leading to a win for the company. Maybe our idea would have prompted a whole new strategy for the company to pursue. We'll never know, because we were too cowardly to share it, telling ourselves that it "wasn't our job".

Senior leaders also succumb to mediocrity due to "it's not my job" thinking. One client of mine, Michael, was the CFO at a hard-charging technology startup. In the course of his work, he saw firsthand that several top executives – the heads of sales, legal and HR – were performing poorly. All were C players whose poor decision-making, lousy attitudes and bad habits were dragging the company down. Michael could have chosen to approach the CEO of the firm, Chuck, with his concerns, recommending that Chuck replace the three executives. But he hadn't yet done that. He'd told himself it wasn't *his* job as CFO to help make those personnel decisions. But that wasn't the real reason he'd failed to act. The real reason was fear. He knew that Chuck had a long-standing friendship with the head of the legal department and would be reluctant to fire him. He was afraid to have a difficult, potentially contentious conversation with Chuck.

Technically, Michael was responsible for running the finance team, raising capital and managing the company's money. But in a broader sense, his job didn't end there; none of ours does. We all bear responsibility for contributing to the general success of the organizations that employ us. We're responsible for adding the most value we can and for refraining from engaging in activities that erode value.

That's our job, in addition to whatever specific duties we signed up to perform. Of course, we can't take direct responsibility for doing everything ourselves. That's not realistic, and if we try to do so, we'll only wind up reducing our ability to add value. But if problems arise, we can't just ignore them. We at least have a duty to help others around us arrive at solutions.

In Michael's case, the CFO's duties gave him a valuable line of sight on the organization. Because he knew the numbers, he could spot when teams or individuals weren't working efficiently. It very much was Michael's job to overcome his fears and raise his concerns with Chuck. Instead of sinking into a comfortable mediocrity, he needed to speak up definitively and behave like an Exceptional kind of leader. With a bit of coaching from me, he eventually did. He came to realize that he was behaving in a mediocre way by keeping his concerns to himself. He found a way of communicating his concerns that Chuck could hear, leading to positive change in the leadership ranks.

Not only does "It's not my job" lead us to do less for our organizations on account of our cowardice, it thwarts our career development. So many people I know claim to be dissatisfied at work. When I ask why, they complain about the company culture: it's too competitive. Or impersonal. Or indecisive. Or bureaucratic.

"Okay," I say, "so what are you doing about it? Have you ever shared ideas about how to improve the culture?"

"Well, no," they reply. "Why would I do that?"

"Because it's your job," I say.

"No, it isn't. My job is to create spreadsheets."

"No," I say. "It's to create spreadsheets *and* to contribute to your company's overall success."

We have the power to serve as change agents, but we don't because we're afraid. That's on us. If we choose to behave in mediocre ways, over time we'll have mediocre careers that leave us dissatisfied. It's as simple as that.

But the converse is also true. When I was twenty-four and working at Interep, I wanted to go to business school but lacked the means. Our company didn't offer tuition reimbursement as a benefit. I could have just accepted that status quo, reasoning that it wasn't my job to change it. Instead, I decided to speak up, admittedly for my own benefit but also for the company's. I probably wasn't the only young employee who wanted to go to business school. If the company had a programme in place to provide support, it would be able to retain more up-and-coming talent.

One day when our chairman was visiting, I walked into the office where he was sitting, introduced myself and proposed that the company pay to send me to business school. In exchange, I'd agree to work for five years afterward. The chairman was so impressed by my proactive thinking and my courage in approaching him that he offered to let me work directly with him for the next two years. If I didn't think that that was the best possible business education, then, yes, he'd send me to business school.

That encounter proved pivotal for me. Over the next two years, I worked for the chairman and had professional experiences that far transcended anything my peers at the company were doing. I gained incredible visibility and moved quickly up the ranks, to the point where people at the company began calling me Doogie Howser, after the famous television character who was a precocious physician. It *was* my job to find growth opportunities for myself within the company and, if they didn't already exist, to take a risk and push for them. Because I transcended mediocrity in that instance, I reaped incredible rewards. And no, I never did wind up getting my MBA during my younger years.

Do you fall back on "it's not my job" thinking? If so, I have just the tool for you. It's called, you guessed it, "It's My Job". This one harkens back to another tool we encountered earlier, "It's My Fault". Take a few minutes and tell yourself all the things that it's your job to do, however ridiculous they might seem. "It's my job to make sure we have enough paper in the supply closet." "It's my job to make sure that we don't waste electricity." "It's my job to make sure our clients get great customer service." "It's my job to make sure that each of my colleagues feels just a little happier and more welcome." And on and on. The point is to train yourself, in a lighthearted way, to think expansively about your responsibility. Again, I don't want you to feel compelled to perform every last task yourself. Rather, I want you to see your job differently and collaborate with others to solve a wider range of problems, saving time and fuelling your own growth.

If you're an assistant and you apply the "It's My Job" tool, you might be more inclined to step up and spend an extra two hours of your day filling in for a colleague who's out on vacation. Others around you will notice the initiative you're taking and recognize you for it, perhaps allowing you to get promoted more quickly. If you're an executive and others around you see you boldly taking responsibility for solving problems that don't technically fit into your area of responsibility, they'll start to do that, too.

To think "It's My Job" is to adopt an Exceptional mindset. Don't wait for others to solve glaring problems. Take the initiative. Use your creativity. Get shit done. Be courageous. People who operate in an Ordinary way do none of this – and it hurts them. Taking responsibility also saves time. Instead of wasting hours on useless arguments about who bears responsibility for tackling an issue, you help drive toward solutions.

Own Your Mediocrity

My point in raising questions about mediocrity and "it's not my job" thinking isn't to be harsh but rather to get you to look squarely at your behaviour. I do this all the time and I find that it benefits my growth tremendously.

That time when I refrained from implementing a strategic plan for my company because I feared the blowback, I was as mediocre as can be. I own that! The point in calling this conduct "mediocre" isn't to dwell on it and feel badly; it's to recognize my lack of courage in a lighthearted way and resolve to do better next time. In that case, I learned that I needed to be decisive even when it's uncomfortable to do so, not cover my own behind. I won't make the same mistake again. Today, I look back on that situation and laugh to myself at how mediocre I was. In the future, I might make some other mediocre move. But not this one.

I'll never forget the moment I first thought of the Line of Mediocrity. I was working with two of my first coaching clients, Matt and Isabella, executives we've met in previous chapters. Each of them had been complaining to me about the other, yet each was too scared to confront the other with their feelings. Their inability to speak openly and boldly was creating a massively dysfunctional environment. Tension was high, and their colleagues were being pulled into a fruitless and time-consuming funk of gossip and commiseration.

It dawned on me that the best way to help fix the situation would be to haul Matt and Isabella into a room and prompt them to speak openly with each other, with me mediating. I don't know what got into me, but when I did that, I started the conversation by saying, "Both of you are mediocre. How are you going to fix it?"

What happened next was incredible. They became defensive, protesting that they weren't mediocre and – to my astonishment – defending the other's honour. "Matt's not mediocre," Isabella said. "He's good at what he does." Matt said something similar about Isabella. Just an hour earlier, those two executives had been at each other's throats, grousing to me about how downright awful the other was. Now they were arguing the exact opposite, because they perceived that I had attacked them.

I sat there for about six or seven minutes, listening and chuckling to myself. When they stopped to ask me what was so funny, I wondered aloud why neither of them had bothered to ask me to define what I meant by mediocre. That took the air out of their balloons. They realized that I'd tricked them in some way. Right then and there, the idea of the Line of Mediocrity came to me. I drew it for them on a piece of paper, pointing out the little bubbles for "good" and "mediocre" right above and below the line.

"Here's what I find interesting," I said. "You guys are both acting below the line because you're eroding your 25th hour by constantly complaining about each other. You're doing nothing to solve it. You're being as Ordinary as Ordinary can be." I went on to describe what Exceptional would look like in their situation. Instead of stewing over a perceived shortcoming or failure on the other's part, they would raise the issue directly and in a respectful way with the other person, approaching from a position of curiosity. "Hey, Matt," Isabella would say, "I don't understand why your department failed to do what you promised. Can you please help me understand?" And Matt would say, "Isabella, you're completely right. We screwed this one up. I'm going to learn from it, and it won't happen again."

Upon hearing that, the two had an epiphany: they *had* been mediocre. And damn, it was funny! They had huge smiles on their faces, realizing how ridiculously they'd been behaving. They respected each other professionally, but because they hadn't known how to communicate openly and courageously, they'd become mired in anger, resentment, and conflict.

Turning to Matt, Isabella repeated the words I'd just scripted for her to raise an issue. Matt responded in the way I'd scripted for him. And just like that, they made the leap from mediocre to good, on their way to Exceptional. The entire conversation took all of ten minutes. It probably saved dozens, even hundreds of hours that they would have spent continuing to fight during the weeks that followed.

Best of all, the conversation wasn't heavy or painful. It didn't cause Matt and Isabella to ruminate on their past behaviour to the point where they went home suffering from a major-league case of the Ucks. It was light, joyful and in the end, fun. Those two acknowledged their mediocrity, but they knew it didn't have to define them. They could change their behaviour and enjoy a better, more productive relationship, moving closer to a 25th hour.

Become Courageous *Today*

Once you start working on your mediocrity and working toward being Exceptional, something wonderful happens: achieving Exceptional becomes *easier*, and you can muster it even when you mess up.

A few years ago, I made a mistake during a meeting, speaking too aggressively to the company's controlling shareholder and CEO, Jimmy, in my capacity as board chairman. Almost immediately after the meeting ended, I realized my error. I'd become upset. I hadn't used my tools. It was totally my fault.

Earlier in my career, when I hadn't had as many tools handy and hadn't been as adept at using them, I might have stewed over that for days. It never would have occurred to me to approach Jimmy and apologize, acknowledging my mistake; that would have been too uncomfortable. As it happened, I still did stew for hours. But then, using my tools to refocus, I realized that I needed to fix it. So I did.

The next morning, I approached Jimmy and apologized. When I first walked into his office, he was frowning and seemed tense, but I didn't hesitate – I launched right into it. "Instead of approaching you in a humble way," I said, "I behaved in a way that must have felt disrespectful. That wasn't my intention, but it happened. I sincerely apologize. My passion got the better of me and I lost my way."

Upon his hearing that, his whole body relaxed. Jimmy told me that he'd been very upset about the situation, so much so that it had kept him up the previous night. But my apology made all the difference.

"I can't tell you how much I appreciate you coming back and owning your mistake," he said. "Thank you."

If I'd responded in a more common, mediocre way, my relationship with Jimmy would have taken a hit, and we'd each have wasted time stressing over the situation and commiserating with others about it. Since I was able to muster courage quickly, I was able not only to rectify the situation but to spread positive vibes to Jimmy. My apology likely left him in a better mood that day, prompting him to spread positivity to others in his orbit.

Traditional therapists and coaches often spend time and energy delving into the past, usually in an attempt to figure out the origins of specific behaviours. I don't focus on any of that. The past is the past. It doesn't matter if you weren't courageous yesterday. When it comes to your growth and development, what I care about is that you'll be courageous *today* and from here on out.

So, yes, laugh at your past mediocrity. Chuckle at how ridiculous you were being. Who cares? It really is kind of funny. And starting today, you can commit to becoming more Exceptional than ever. You can manage *yourself* better, claiming a spot high above the Line of Mediocrity. And when you backslide, as you inevitably will, you can laugh at that, too.

Find Your 25th Hour: Line of Mediocrity

Looking back on your career and personal life, think of three times when you behaved in a mediocre way. Maybe you failed to speak up in a meeting when you had an idea. Maybe you failed to have a difficult conversation with a friend or colleague. Maybe you failed to step up and make a bold decision as a leader for fear of possible blowback. For each situation, consider how you would handle it differently today. What would you say or do to better rise to the occasion? Keeping those moments fresh in your mind can serve as a reminder to behave more courageously as you face new situations. Challenge yourself to soar way above the line of mediocrity – because you can!

Fourteen

Trust Yourself So That You Can Trust and Lead Others

While we're talking about courage, I have a tool that will require every ounce of it you've got. Okay, I'm being dramatic. But here it is: each day for three weeks, I want you to set aside ten minutes at the worst possible time to do *absolutely nothing*. When I say "the worst possible time", I mean you're about to have a big board meeting in an hour or your final interview for the big job you want or a critical meeting with your team or a big college exam, and you don't feel prepared. By "do *absolutely nothing*", I mean that you are to stare out of the window and say to yourself, "Well, it's raining, and – oh, look, the flowers are beginning to bloom." You set a timer, and for exactly ten minutes, you don't think about work, your to-do list or anything pressing in your personal life. You think about nothing.

This tool, which is called "Ten Minutes a Day", causes my clients to lose their minds. They find it exquisitely painful to "waste" ten minutes when they feel they most need that time, and they fear that they'll be dooming themselves to failure in their upcoming endeavour.

One client of mine, a highly accomplished executive named Lydia, found "Ten Minutes a Day" to be "superhard" and also "the most annoying" of all of my tools. For weeks, she couldn't make it for even four minutes. "My head kept veering into different thoughts and how much I had to do," she said. But she kept at it, and eventually, "it just clicked".

Years later, Lydia uses "Ten Minutes a Day" as a kind of extended version of "Pause Button". She reflects that taking those ten minutes to do nothing taught her how to clear her head, removing all the noise so that she could go at problems with a new perspective. She'd long felt enormous stress in her job and had got into the habit of behaving reactively to get things done. Now when she feels overwhelmed, she has a tool that lets her step outside it all, take a breather and start fresh.

Although I'm glad Lydia has found "Ten Minutes a Day" useful in this way, I designed the tool with a different purpose in mind, one that my clients find surprising. Most of them presume that "Ten Minutes a Day" is about time management, and on a superficial level, it is. When you force yourself to do nothing for a full ten minutes, you gain more appreciation for all that you *could* be doing. Used efficiently, ten minutes is a significant block of time. You could skim through dozens of emails or plan your activities for the rest of the day. You could conduct a quick morning check-in with your team, arrange for a plumber to fix a broken faucet in your house, or review financials for one of your big accounts. As you learn just how valuable ten minutes is, you become less inclined to waste it, and that motivates you to move toward a 25th hour.

But there's a deeper and more significant point to "Ten Minutes a Day": when you experiment with this tool, I'm guessing that you'll wind up completing the stressful task on your plate just fine. Probably you'll perform way above your expectations. What does that teach you? It's this: although you feared "wasting" those ten minutes during that stressful time, you didn't need them. You *were* prepared for that big meeting, conversation or exam; you just didn't *feel* that you were ready. You didn't trust yourself. And that's what needs to change.

The Importance of Trust

Learning to trust ourselves and our capabilities is essential if we want to claim a 25th hour. Think of all the time we spend preparing for our presentations and meetings. Most of that is probably overpreparation. My clients overprepare all the time, probably by a factor of two, three or more. They do so because they're gripped by fear. They're freaked out about the possibility of failure. That's because they don't believe in their own power. They don't trust themselves.

This lack of trust – in both ourselves and others – can be even more problematic for leaders, contributing to what I can only describe as an epidemic of micromanaging. One study found that leaders wasted almost seven hours each week on tasks that they could have paid other people to take off their plates.[1] Camilla, a midlevel head of marketing whom I mentor, is a case in point. When we first met, she was extremely talented but struggled when it came to delegating tasks to others. Seeing herself as a strong contributor, she presumed that she could accomplish tasks better and faster than her team members could. Through our work together, she came to see that she wasn't placing enough trust in her team members to get the job done and that her lack of trust was dragging down the team's performance. She was spending endless hours on tasks that others could have done. She lacked time to focus on higher-value strategic issues, and she went through her days feeling constantly overworked and stressed. Meanwhile, her team members weren't getting the opportunities they needed to learn and grow.

Camilla and I pondered the question of *why* she wasn't trusting others. It wasn't that her team members weren't trustworthy. Rather, she hadn't developed the capacity to trust them. It might seem counterintuitive, but before we can trust others, we must first develop a strong, abiding trust in ourselves. We must believe in our own capacities and, most importantly, in our ability to manage ourselves using the kinds of tools presented in this book.

Delegating tasks to others requires that we give up some degree of control over the outcome. People might mess something up, or they might perform tasks in ways that aren't exactly as we would have done them. When we trust others, we're implicitly trusting ourselves to sort out and fix any unexpected problems that might arise, feeling confident that we have the tools, skills and expertise required. More importantly, we're trusting that we can manage ourselves emotionally by using the tools in this book, handling the discomfort of being exposed to novel and unfamiliar solutions, and staying calm in the face of unexpected setbacks.

I once worked with a colleague in his late twenties, Randy, to create presentations for an executive leadership retreat at a company I helped lead. We planned that I'd guide those senior leaders through a neat little role-playing exercise that would help them learn important communication skills. But when it came time for the exercise, I threw our plans out the window. It occurred to me that Randy would benefit by getting the chance to lead it. So on the spur of the moment and without giving him any warning, I asked him to do so.

Randy was younger and less experienced than many of the participants, and he'd never led a portion of a retreat before. He was surprised, to say the least, that I was handing control of the proceedings over to him. I couldn't be sure that he'd rise to the occasion. But he did. Afterward, he remarked that the experience had helped him gain confidence in his ability to perform well in a high-pressure professional situation. Because I'd trusted in him, he was able to trust himself.

But I was able to trust Randy and delegate that task only because I trusted in my own capability to navigate the results, whatever they turned out to be. Perhaps Randy would take a much different approach to the exercise than I would. I felt comfortable plunging into that uncertainty. I knew that I was skilled enough at managing myself to handle any situation that might arise. My self-confidence as a leader translated into a learning opportunity for Randy, and it also moved me closer to a 25th hour. I gained back the time I would have spent leading the exercise. I could have used those minutes any way I liked, but I chose to participate in the exercise. That allowed me to spend precious moments observing other leaders on the team and learning more about their personalities and communication prowess.

I'm not claiming that I'm *always* this adept at trusting myself and in turn delegating to others. Although I've been working on it for years, I still slip up, especially at home. I'm the kind of person who likes a house to be neat and orderly. My wife can tolerate a bit more disorder. Sometimes she'll put papers down on a table in our front hallway, and they'll stay there for several days. When I see them, I erode my 25th hour in a couple of ways. First, I waste time obsessing over how disorganized my wife is and how messy those papers look. Second, rather than waiting for my wife to put the papers away on her own time, I eventually take time to do so myself. It's a classic case of micromanaging, replicated every day in homes and workplaces everywhere.

In truth, there's no right or wrong way to keep a house. My wife's approach is just as good as mine. I'm not *trusting* her to put the papers away on her own time and in her own way. And that's because in an important sense, I don't trust myself in this situation to deal with the uncertainty and discomfort. My Devil takes over, in the form of fear of the unknown and of potential discomfort. How long will those papers sit there? Will the room seem too cluttered? Will it upset me if it does? Will I obsess about it even more? These concerns freak me out enough to want to put the papers away myself. In effect, I'm not trusting my ability to manage my own emotions so that I won't waste time feeling stressed out and obsessing about those papers. If I did have that trust, I'd be able to give my wife more space.

Trust in ourselves comes naturally as we work with and master the tools. The better we get at managing ourselves generally, the better able we are to tolerate uncertainty and novelty without feeling so much fear. We can take a deep breath and let others take more control, potentially making mistakes and learning in the process. Practising "Ten Minutes a Day" reinforces these efforts to build trust in ourselves. At the very moment when we're feeling the most stress, we remind ourselves that yes, we can have faith in our own capabilities. We take ourselves out of a fear-based, reactive mindset and allow ourselves to operate in a way that is clearer and more self-possessed. We become more creative and open to new possibilities that others present to us.

Of Ice Cream and Lessons Learned

As you work with your tools to build self-trust and in turn trust in others, let me share two other, supportive tools that can help you feel more comfortable delegating tasks and opening space for others to operate in. The first, called "Ice Cream Store", dates from when I was in my late twenties and working at Interep. Back then, I didn't trust myself as I (usually) do now. It was killing me and dragging down my team. I wasn't a despotic micromanager who shouted out commands and tore into team members who didn't perform tasks to my specifications. Rather, I had a more polite, passive-aggressive style. If someone took on a project and injected a bit of individuality into it, I'd softly redirect them to do it as *I* would have done it, saying something such as, "Yeah, that way you did the project was good. But what if we did it this way?" I couldn't let go enough to let my team members be creative and shine. Although I didn't realize it, I was holding them back, and I was eroding my 25th hour by spending way too much time overseeing and directing them.

I woke up to my lack of trust one weekend when my team was working on a project for a major movie studio. I didn't trust that they would do it correctly – that is, in a way that was familiar to and comfortable for me. My fears became so great that I wound up staying up until 3:00 am that Saturday night doing work that one of my account executives was supposed to do. While I finished the task, staring at my 1990s-era computer screen, it occurred to bleary-eyed me how ridiculous I was being. Rather than enjoying the weekend, I would spend much of the next day catching up on sleep. On Monday, when I presented what I'd done to the team, they'd feel crappy, realizing that I hadn't trusted them to do their jobs correctly.

Those thoughts prompted a visual to pop up in my mind. Have you ever seen those ice cream bars that have three flavours in one – vanilla, chocolate and strawberry? When I was a kid, they were the standard fare at birthday parties, and I used to hate them. I don't like chocolate, so I'd have to spend time and effort eating around it. It was a pain, and to top it off, I left one-third of the ice cream behind. But there was another reason I couldn't stand those ice cream bars: they were freaking *boring*. Vanilla, chocolate and strawberry. Over and over again. Vanilla, chocolate and strawberry. Hadn't people heard of peanut butter crunch? Or cookies and cream? Or a million other flavours?

I realized that by micromanaging, I was limiting my team's creative possibilities. The way *I* liked to do things was tantamount to the standard vanilla-chocolate-strawberry. If I let go a little and trusted my team members, they might come up with new solutions that I'd never tried but that would be totally amazing. Those solutions might be the equivalent of peanut butter fudge swirl. Blueberry passionfruit sorbet. French vanilla elderflower. Flavours with individuality, just like each of us.

My "Ice Cream Store" tool is simple: if you're a leader, don't just refrain from micromanaging and imposing solutions; challenge your team members to come up with new "flavours" when delivering work to you. Ask them to find their own *unique* flavour or way of performing a task and give them bonus points for arriving at a flavour that you've never tried before. When they come back with a novel solution, resist the urge to judge it immediately. Instead, give it a try. Take out one of those little plastic spoons and take a taste of it. You might hate it and think that your standard vanilla-chocolate-strawberry is better. Or you might find a new flavour or way of doing something that becomes your new favourite.

If you wind up hating a novel solution that your team members produce, a second tool up my sleeve will come in handy. This one is inspired by an experience I had back in kindergarten. At the end of the year, my school put on a graduation ceremony, and my mum went out and bought me a new suit to wear for the occasion. About an hour before we were supposed to leave for the ceremony, I put on my new suit and then sat around looking for something to do. I decided to go outside and play in the backyard. When my mum called me back inside so that we could leave, she was shocked and angered to see that I'd got big, ugly grass stains all over my new suit.

Unfortunately, I didn't have another suit, so I had to clean off the outfit as best I could and wear it. When I showed up at school, my suit still looked terrible, and all the other kids made fun of me. The embarrassment I felt stuck with me. To this day, decades later, if I have an event coming up and I'm wearing nice clothes, I'll take great care not to get them dirty. If I'm out at a restaurant on a business lunch, I'll sometimes even tuck a napkin into my collar and wear it over my shirt to protect my tie. Yes, it looks ridiculous, but I don't care. I made a mistake, and I've learned my lesson.

My tool, which I call "Mistakes Made and Lessons Learned", entails making a list, preferably a lengthy one, of mistakes you've made during your life and the important lessons you've learned as a result. Start with the biggest mistakes and life lessons, but also include some smaller ones that continue to shape your behaviour and decision-making. You forgot to study for an exam until the last minute and got a C. From that you learned to start studying at least a week before.

Write that one down. When you've made your list, pin it up in your office or somewhere else where you'll see it. Keep some empty space at the bottom of the list. As you make new mistakes and learn new lessons, write them in.

This tool reminds you how important it is to make mistakes for the sake of your growth and development. Everyone has a collection of mistakes they've made and lessons they've learned. The longer we live, the bigger that collection is. I'm in my mid-fifties, and I must have a walk-in closet full of mistakes and lessons. If we remind ourselves of this reality, we can be more forgiving of mistakes our team members make when we delegate tasks to them. This leaves us more comfortable giving them space to be themselves.

More than that, we can focus on frequently creating opportunities for team members to take on new challenges precisely so that they can make mistakes and grow. I did that with Randy. While he didn't make any mistakes that time, he has on other occasions, and that's perfectly fine. As a leader, I helped him build his collection of mistakes and lessons so that he can develop both competency in his work and an underlying trust in himself. Someday, with any luck, he'll have a storage closet full of mistakes made and lessons learned just as I do.

Consider the Worst Thing

I'm not saying that leaders must abandon oversight entirely and delegate *everything* to inexperienced team members. Doing so would of course be reckless and reflect poor judgment on our part. When creating space for others to learn and grow, we must recognize that some potential mistakes are minor, while others can cause enormous damage. Delegate when mistakes are likely to be minor and able to be repaired without much cost or difficulty, taking into account as well the benefits that might arise in terms of learning and new ideas. If the mistakes will have serious consequences for the team, organization or individual employee, refrain from delegating.

"What's the Worst Thing That Can Happen?" can help us here. When I decided to let Randy lead participants through an exercise for the first time, I ran through that tool in my mind and concluded that the worst thing that could happen was that he'd mess up the exercise and I'd have to intercede to salvage it. I further calculated that the odds of that happening were extremely low – maybe 2 per cent at best. Delegating to Randy in that instance and giving him an opportunity to showcase his skills was a no-brainer. As it turned out, he did a great job, and he did so with the equivalent of his own unique flavour of ice cream. It wasn't a flavour that I would have chosen, yet it was still fantastic.

Team members can often make an impact by injecting their own unique style, judgment or insight. Alan, a CEO I coach, had to decide what to do with an executive named Kenneth, a difficult personality who in the past had spawned conflict inside the company. Alan's first inclination was to fire Kenneth, but a member of his team, Melinda, had a different idea. Having supervised Kenneth in the past, she wanted to assign him to a new role. She went to Alan insisting that that was the right decision and asking Alan to let her make the call. Alan was annoyed. Although he respected Melinda's judgment, he didn't see what sense it would possibly make to keep Kenneth in the company instead of firing him.

Alan wondered if he would do well to delegate the decision to Melinda even though he "knew" that her preference was the wrong one. We ran through "What's the Worst Thing That Can Happen?" together. In Alan's mind, the worst thing that could happen was that Kenneth would fail once again in that new role and the company would have to fire him. Given Kenneth's past behaviour, Alan pegged the chance of this happening at a relatively high 40 per cent. Still, as he saw, this outcome, if it materialized, wouldn't be so bad. The company wouldn't lose any revenue or customers, and it wouldn't suffer any reputational damage. Reassigning Kenneth might turn out to be a mistake, but it would be a minor and survivable one.

Alan delegated the decision to Melinda. And lo and behold, she was right! Kenneth thrived in his new position. He had been talented and a good hire all along, but his prior position had been an awful fit for him. Because Alan had delegated the decision to Melinda, the company saved the time and money it would have spent firing Kenneth and hiring and training his replacement. Melinda came away feeling that Alan had trusted her, and that helped her feel more trusting of herself. Alan's way of looking at Kenneth's situation had been the equivalent of vanilla-chocolate-strawberry. Kenneth hadn't worked out in his first job, so the standard operating move was to fire him. Melinda looked at the situation differently, the equivalent of, say, salted caramel peanut butter. And it turned out that Alan did indeed like the way that tasted.

I'm making myself hungry and probably you, too, so I'd better bring this chapter to a close. Here's a final thought: many leaders believe that team members and others around them must earn their trust. That's a tough, pragmatic-sounding thing to say. In truth, it's entirely Ordinary. Leaders who are Exceptional and who operate far above the Line of Mediocrity make extending trust the *default* position. From the moment they meet a new team member, they're looking for opportunities to delegate and let them shine. They run through "What's the Worst Thing That Can Happen?", but once they see that a potential mistake wouldn't be too damaging, they let it rip. That's how deep their commitment to others' learning runs. That's how much they understand the value of delegation. And that's how intensely they trust *themselves* and their ability to manage through uncertainty and unfamiliarity.

To advance your own growth and development, don't focus on whether others "deserve" your trust; focus on your own capacity to bestow it. Enlarge that capacity by continuing to work with your tools. If you do, I promise you that those ten minutes you spend looking out the window and thinking of nothing will save you untold hours, while earning you the gratitude, loyalty and respect of your team members and others in your life.

Find Your 25th Hour: Ice Cream Store

I've discussed how leaders can use "Ice Cream Store" with their teams, but you can also use it with yourself. Make a list of key tasks you performed at work over the past week. These might include leading the regular team check-in, holding performance reviews, following up on a customer issue or holding a project meeting with fellow students. Think about how you approached these tasks: did you do so in a rote way, or did you find ways to inject your own individuality and flavour into them? For each task, challenge yourself to find at least one way to do something a little different in a way that is uniquely *you*.

Fifteen

Nurture Vulnerability

Now that we've covered topics such as self-confidence, courage and trust, I'm going to unveil one of the flat-out ballsiest tools I've ever created. I designed it with leaders in mind, but any of us can use it to help people around us resolve disputes and function better as a team.

I call this tool "Who Can I Blame?". Yep, we're going there. Let's say you have two or more people or groups of people who aren't getting along and have been quietly undermining one another. Rather than letting that tension continue to fester, bring the antagonistic parties together around a table, placing them on opposite sides so that they're facing each other. You want them to be right up in each other's grills.

But you also want to keep the tone light, removing the stigma around the concept of blame or fault. To that end, you might start this exercise by taking people through "It's My Fault", which I discussed in chapter 5. On the surface, these two tools might appear contradictory, but please stay with me to learn how they can work together. Once you've introduced "It's My Fault", after the group has loosened up a little, ask each person to create a list of their grievances. For each one, participants must identify a person in the room by name whom they blame. When everyone is ready with their list, go around and ask each person to make their grievances public, including naming names. It's time to get real, folks. Nobody defends themselves yet; we're just airing gripes and blaming people.

If people have duplicate gripes, they are to refrain from repeating them and air only ones that others haven't yet articulated. As the facilitator, keep the gripes coming and make them visible to everyone by compiling a list on a whiteboard. If you lack a whiteboard, a notebook will work just fine. Once everyone's gripes are on the table, ask members of each group to discuss items on the list for which others have blamed them. Give the accusers the chance to elaborate on their gripes, resolving any confusion or lack of clarity. Give the accused a chance to clarify their intent and acknowledge ways in which they really did mess up. Allow for some back-and-forth. When appropriate, encourage the participants to create plans to address ongoing problems.

You might think that an exercise such as this is a recipe for a reality TV–style blowup. That could be true, depending on the personalities involved, so you'll need to apply some judgment. If people on your team are too immature or antagonistic to engage in such an open and honest conversation, you might decide to modify the exercise. But most likely they can handle it and just need some prodding from you to make themselves vulnerable enough to speak freely. In that case, mustering a bit of courage yourself and organizing a "Who Can I Blame?" session can make an enormous difference, cutting through conflict that might have gobbled up enormous amounts of time.

Vulnerability in Action

I saw the impact that "Who Can I Blame?" can have while working with two groups at a technology company. One group was an eight-person sales team, the other a twelve-person product team charged with making custom software. The two departments had a history of bad blood. The product people thought that the members of the sales team were phoning it in and not meeting goals as outlined in the company's strategic plan. The sales team thought that the product delivery folks were incompetent and unable to deliver the sophisticated software applications the company was trying to sell.

For many months, the conflict bubbled beneath the surface. Members of each group commiserated about how crappy the other was, but they were too afraid and Ordinary to talk directly to members of the other group to air their concerns and resolve their disagreements. The company was missing its revenue goals, and people on both teams were seeing serious erosion of their 25th hour.

Conducting "Who Can I Blame?" with those teams took about two hours, plus another half hour of time that I spent organizing it. During the first hour, I collected over fifty accusations, a majority of them generated by the product team because of its larger size. Some interesting grievances came up. A senior person on the product team accused certain salespeople of wasting their time going to trade shows and partying with customers. Another product guy resented the fact that salespeople didn't consult with his team when creating their sales strategies.

Meanwhile, salespeople felt that individual colleagues on the product side had little faith in them, which had sent their morale plummeting. They also thought that key product developers were way too bureaucratic and slow in meeting the market demand, and that they were insular and didn't communicate very well about their projected delivery dates.

Once those gripes had been aired, I helped the two teams talk through them one by one. We dispensed quickly with several of the grievances, since they involved misunderstandings or complaints about an individual's behaviour that they could easily fix. Addressing the accusation that they were partying too much, members of the sales team reminded their product-side colleagues that socializing with clients and prospective clients was their job. As they explained, their trips to trade shows weren't fun and games. They were exhausting, since they entailed long days of sales meetings. The frequent travel was stressful, taking them away from their families. As one sales lead explained, prospective customers might have ordered alcoholic beverages, but he and his colleagues ordered iced tea. Members of the product team empathized with their sales colleagues and admitted that they'd been too quick to judge. Appreciating how hard the sales team was working, they apologized and agreed never to raise the issue again.

Some of the grievances involved process changes and so were harder to resolve. Members of the product team acknowledged that they were sometimes slower than they liked to get new software out the door, especially when it came to custom orders. We spent some time brainstorming changes they could make to speed up their process without compromising quality or adding new costs. The teams also discussed how sales could consult better with their product-side colleagues in designing their strategies and how the product team could communicate better.

By the end of the two hours, the teams had crafted detailed plans for solving those issues. Even more promising, I noticed, was an overall change in tone. Unfounded anger and resentment melted away, replaced by mutual understanding, forgiveness and excitement. The conversation became lighthearted as people recognized how silly some of their misconceptions about their colleagues had been. After the exercise, a number of participants approached me to express how meaningful the experience had been for them. It felt scary at first to be so direct and honest with their colleagues, but it was such a relief to finally express what they'd been thinking and feeling. Most of all, they found it wonderful to repair dysfunctional relationships and feel closer to their colleagues on the other team.

"Who Can I Blame?" was a big win for those colleagues. Members of the two teams went on to save enormous amounts of time because they'd built the capacity to express criticisms and resentments as they were brewing, catching them before they festered. They felt more comfortable owning up to weaknesses and mistakes and openly discussing work experiences both positive and negative. Ultimately, the experience taught them to become more *vulnerable* with one another, to let down their guard and express their feelings and opinions. That vulnerability would help them resolve issues more quickly and prevent tensions from deepening, catapulting them toward a 25th hour.

The Power of Being Yourself

The best-selling psychologist and author Brené Brown has described how a willingness to make ourselves vulnerable, expressing ourselves authentically warts and all, can help us feel more worthy and develop "a strong sense of love and belonging". Brown conceives of vulnerability as the ability to "tell the story of who you are with your whole heart" and in particular as having "the courage to be imperfect".[1] Vulnerability, as I see it, includes a willingness to swallow hard and tell others what we *really* think, including negative thoughts, perceptions and feelings we might have as issues arise. But it's more than that. When we overcome our fears and open ourselves up to others, we offer them a glimpse into our raw humanity, sharing our flaws, struggles and disappointments. As we become Exceptional leaders, we reveal our own struggles to manage ourselves better using the tools presented in this book. Part of managing our own emotions is in fact learning how to feel comfortable letting others in on that ongoing work.

In the workplace, allowing for more self-disclosure leads to the kinds of emotional benefits Brown described, but it also has some hugely practical ones. If we give into our fears and erect a facade of perfection, as so many professionals do, purporting to know everything, it won't be long before we fail. But if we walk into a room and say, "Hey, I've got a problem. I'm stuck. I don't know what to do and would love your help on it," our colleagues will likely do everything in their power to help us with it, and they'll also show us more vulnerability themselves. All of us save ourselves the song and dance that we typically do to show how "in control" we are. That charade gets us nowhere, serving simply to distract us from addressing the real problems we need to solve.

I'm not suggesting that we let our boundaries fall away and divulge everything. If we dwell unduly on our weaknesses and insecurities, we risk distracting our colleagues and turning work into an ongoing therapy session. We don't need others at work to know gory details about, say, our upcoming colonoscopy or our recent romantic breakup. We also don't need to share resentments or negative thoughts that don't bear on the work at hand. But honestly revealing ourselves is a more fulfilling and efficient way of doing business. We can accomplish more if we show others that we're human and trust them to deal with us compassionately and helpfully.

Leading with Vulnerability

If we lead others, showing vulnerability becomes both more important – and more difficult. We have an opportunity to model this behaviour for other team members, helping an entire group become more expressive, honest and open. But we might also have stronger internal barriers that prevent us from opening up. Quite often, our robot tells us that to get promoted, we must present ourselves as bosses who are hardened and tough. It tells us that others are watching us and we must "play the part" of the authoritative, unflappable leader. Although traditional identities have come into question, many men still grow up believing that they shouldn't express their emotions or talk about their feelings. If they do, they're "weak", inviting others in competitive work environments to walk all over them. As male leaders continue to frame their behaviour around such beliefs, their lack of vulnerability can become a cultural norm, making female leaders more reluctant to open up for fear of appearing "soft".

I often coach leaders who struggle to acknowledge their true feelings and share them with others. I was in a session recently with a client, and he mentioned that a previous session we'd had together had been extremely difficult for him. When I asked why, he talked a lot but didn't really give me much of an answer. So I asked him again; same non-response. "Focus on the truth right now," I said. "Remember, I am the safest professional resource you will ever have. Why was our session last time really so hard?"

He thought about it for a moment. "The truth is," he said, "I was embarrassed." When I asked why, he told me that I'd explained something to him and it had taken him a really long time to understand it. "It was really hard for me because I was wondering, why am I not getting this concept? Why doesn't this stuff come more naturally to me?"

I smiled. "Do you know how amazing it is that you just told the truth by using the word 'embarrassed'?"

He shook his head. "No, no, you're missing my point. That's not what I'm talking about."

"You're missing my point," I said. "That's precisely what we're talking about."

I push leaders so insistently on vulnerability because I see what happens when they lack this capacity. When I started coaching Teddy, one of three senior partners at a law firm, he conducted himself in such an impersonal way that he came across to others around him as not merely unengaged but also unhappy. In meetings with his twenty-five-person team, he would sit there with a blank expression on his face, as if he were stoically persevering through a painful visit to the dentist. His apparent misery bothered his team members a great deal, impacting their morale. Although they were trying their hardest, they couldn't seem to please their boss.

When I asked Teddy about his seeming unhappiness, he was shocked and said he didn't feel unhappy at all. Most of the time during meetings, he was just listening and thinking; his stoic look was actually one of contemplation. As we discussed it further, we realized that the negative impressions he was leaving were owed to his lack of vulnerability. For reasons that boiled down to fear, he had got into the habit of bottling himself up at work, leaving his "real self" at the door and cultivating an impenetrable outer shell. If he wanted to become an Exceptional leader, he'd need to loosen up, let his personality shine more, and at appropriate moments be willing to express his true opinions.

Teddy started to work on his vulnerability. At one staff meeting, he kicked off the discussion by saying, "Hey, I want you to know that notwithstanding the expression on my face, I feel friggin' awesome this morning. So, yes, this is my happy face." That got some chuckles and smiles, and it surprised his team. For the first time, he was trusting them enough to let them in. He was not only reassuring them of his positive emotional state but implicitly acknowledging the difficulty he had expressing his emotions. His team felt heard and validated because he'd owned up to a flaw of his and because they understood that he was making an effort to manage himself better around them. Meanwhile, his use of humour lightened the mood, making the conversation fun, not awkward. That attempt at vulnerability took just a few moments, enabling the team to then get serious and address the business at hand.

Within just a few weeks, thanks to a series of moments like that, Teddy saw a marked difference in his team's morale. Whereas before his team members had seemed frustrated and tense, now they appeared energized and happier. Ideas flowed more freely during discussions, new client pitches and deal making improved, and the team got more done, all because Teddy had worked on loosening up and being more human.

Four Vulnerability Tools

Given how difficult it can be to break the sequence and reveal more of yourself, I've developed a collection of relevant tools that I call my vulnerability suite. Let's run through them one by one.

Tool 1: Feedback Is Your Friend

When we fail to show vulnerability, we often have trouble hearing feedback from others, much less taking it. "Feedback Is Your Friend" encourages you to make yourself vulnerable by purposely and regularly soliciting blunt feedback. I learned about this concept at Interep while attending a workshop facilitated by Dr Gerald Bell, a professor at the University of North Carolina who operated the Bell Leadership Institute. The gist of the tool is this: if you're a college student, try going up to a professor and saying, "Hi, Professor, you know what would really help me? Could you please just list three or four things that you *hated* about this paper?"

Having a conversation like this will enable you to get frank feedback from people who otherwise might not have shared it for fear of hurting your feelings. In workplace settings, making yourself vulnerable by asking colleagues or bosses for blunt feedback enables you to surface issues that might have gone unaddressed while also fostering more trust in your relationships. When you acknowledge your limitations, your colleagues and bosses feel more comfortable doing so, too.

Teddy didn't simply work with me to show more humanity with his team; he met individually with about half his team to solicit feedback about his leadership style. He learned that he indeed has a sour look on his face while he's pondering something. It was one thing for me to tell him that, quite another when he heard it repeatedly from colleagues he'd known and respected for years. Not only did he feel more motivated to change; the gesture of asking for blunt feedback was itself a show of vulnerability, marking a clear departure from his past behaviour. By the time he started to poke fun at his cold demeanour in meetings, he had already begun to acknowledge his own flaws with members of his team.

Tool 2: Quick Check-in

As you'll remember from chapter 3, this tool has you start meetings by going around the table and having everyone utter one word that best conveys their current state of mind. Doing so helps you pare back unproductive chatter and make meetings shorter, but it also helps you start each meeting with some personally revealing statements from everyone present, however brief. You implicitly establish personal expression as a norm, opening the way for more authenticity, honesty and humanity. You also gain information that will help avoid misunderstandings and conflict. If someone checks in with a word such as "distracted", "overwhelmed" or "upset", they're owning up to the reality that they have other things on their mind. The rest of the team will understand that they might not be as sensitive or thoughtful as they ordinarily would be.

At a recent meeting at which I facilitated "Quick Check-in", the six team members present checked in as "curious", "frustrated", "focused", "intrigued", "caffeinated" and "organized". The male colleague who checked in as "frustrated" caught my eye. Before launching into the agenda, I asked Mr Frustrated if he'd feel comfortable briefly sharing why he felt that way. It turns out that a miscommunication had occurred, and he was expecting that he'd have to deal with a challenging client issue. The female colleague who checked in as "caffeinated" knew about the situation; she jumped in with a helpful idea for mitigating the issue. Mr Frustrated immediately relaxed and was better able to focus on the current meeting. I learned afterward that Ms Caffeinated's idea had worked well and the issue had been resolved.

If our team hadn't performed vulnerability testing via "Quick Check-in", Mr Frustrated would have suffered for days and possibly weeks, eroding his 25th hour.

Tool 3: The Vulnerability Log

To help track your progress in your ability to express your true feelings, thoughts and experiences, I recommend that you keep a log for a month, recording moments when you did and didn't behave authentically with others. Notice how people around you responded, and log that, too. At the end of the month, review what you wrote. Noticing the times when you could have been more expressive but weren't might spur you to work harder in this area. Your motivation might also increase as you recognize how openness on your part elicited more warmth and humanity from others and how more reserve led others to pull away from you or shut down. As I think you'll discover, vulnerability doesn't weaken you as a leader but rather enables you to build stronger, more trusting connections with your team members.

Tool 4: Adventures in Self-Management

You can get more mileage out of the tools in this book by using them as opportunities to practise vulnerability. Keep track of times when you began to spiral and had to whip out some of your tools to keep your emotions in check or you wish you'd done so. Tell others about it, detailing all that you did to tamp down that nasty Devil. I do this frequently with colleagues and clients, and I've spent a considerable portion of this book fessing up about times when I used my tools to calm myself down or failed to use them and made a mistake.

Not long ago, I had some challenges with a board on which I'm serving, and in the middle of a meeting I became gripped by insecurity and fear that my influence would diminish. Giving myself a cookie didn't work. I had another meeting right after that one, and I didn't want my emotions to bog me down. So on the way to the second meeting, I found an empty conference room, closed the door and spent five or six minutes running through "What's the Worst Thing That Can Happen?". The worst that could happen, I decided, was that I'd suffer a big blow to my ego. I calculated that there was at best a 2 per cent chance of that scenario materializing. Was I going to waste my time focusing on an outcome that had only a 2 per cent chance of happening or use my time well by focusing on one that was 98 per cent likely to occur? Asking myself that question caused my rational brain to click in and drown out my pesky Devil.

Because I'd taken time out to manage myself, I ran late for my second meeting, which I was leading. When I arrived there, I took everyone through the "Quick Check-in". I can't remember the word I used, but it was something like "calmer" or "refocused". I then took a moment to apologize for being late and explain what had happened. I didn't go into detail about the situation that had unnerved me. Rather, I shared with the room that I'd been upset during my previous meeting, that I'd needed to mobilize my toolbox and that I'd used "What's the Worst Thing That Can Happen?" to adjust my thinking.

That little bit of self-disclosure prompted a slew of questions from others in the room. I shared a bit more about my Devil and the kinds of situations that awaken him out of his slumber. My colleagues were intrigued to hear that I, the leader and coach, also have moments when I need to apply my tools. It felt refreshing to them to learn that I was imperfect and experienced emotional turmoil just as they did. That conversation took just a few minutes, and then we went on to have an unusually productive meeting. Afterward, several people approached me to thank me for discussing my situation, telling me that it had helped them feel better about the issues that they were dealing with.

Changing the Tone

When you work over time to behave more authentically around others, the effects can be profound. At the beginning of this book, I referenced a story of a professional whose technical team had failed in its attempt to deliver a new product for a high-profile client. What I didn't tell you was that the failure was a major setback for the company, one that put its future into jeopardy. The setback confronted the CEO, Karl, with a major leadership challenge: how could he inspire his workforce to stick together, work hard and turn the company's prospects around?

Before his business career, Karl had spent years in the military, where he'd been trained in the "don't let them see you sweat" school of leadership. Showing vulnerability had never been his strong suit, and now he doubled down on his authoritative personality, projecting toughness, decisiveness and determination. Ignoring the emotional impact of the setback, he barked out orders like a drill sergeant, telling his team to buck up, quickly put the setback behind them and try harder. Behind closed doors, he was awash in anxiety and self-doubt, yet he diligently hid those emotions, thinking that he was setting an example of "strong", alpha male–style leadership.

In fact, Karl's tough-guy response only made the situation worse. His workforce was upset, worried and demoralized, unsure if they'd have jobs to go to in a few months. Because Karl wasn't acknowledging their negative feelings or his own disappointment and fears, they perceived him as cold and distant. His uncompromising, top-down directives only intensified those impressions, causing his people to clam up because they felt unsafe to express their doubts and insecurities. Tensions rose, teams lost momentum and individual employees wasted time spiralling. The organization wasn't rallying as it needed to for the company to survive.

With my help, Karl pivoted, learning to be more honest with his people about the blow the setback had dealt him. Although it felt uncomfortable, he began to talk in town hall meetings about the fear he was feeling, admitting that the failure had made him question his abilities and noting that others were probably struggling with similar feelings. He explained that even though he was feeling fearful, he remained confident that the company would succeed. He mobilized some key talking points to explain why.

By speaking about his own emotional turmoil, Karl connected with his workforce in a new way. They didn't see him as weak but rather as an imperfect human being with messy feelings just like they had. They admired him more, not less, and felt reassured that the company saw their humanity and would accept and even welcome their flaws and imperfections. Karl's references to his emotional turmoil also made his confidence in the company's future seem more credible. He was feeling the full measure of what had happened, yet he still believed fervently that the company would succeed. That meant something.

By softening his message and making it more personal, Karl inspired his people to do a reset and redouble their efforts. It's not clear whether the company will survive, but with Karl allowing more of his authentic self to peek through, it stands a fighting chance. His employees are far more focused, productive and fired up than ever to succeed.

Expressing vulnerability shifts the tone inside our teams and organizations. It turns cold, businesslike or hostile environments into ones that are warmer, more compassionate and more trusting. That in turn makes for a less conflict-ridden and more productive place to work, moving everyone toward their 25th hour. Ordinary professionals fear sharing anything about themselves. Exceptional leaders fuel their personal and career growth by expressing their authentic thoughts and feelings. They foster a tone that is businesslike and professional, yet also personal. As they know, business is a team sport. Coordinating with others requires that we offer them a glimpse of what we're thinking and feeling. Rather than fleeing from our humanity, we have much to gain by embracing it.

Find Your 25th Hour: Tracking Your Tone

What tone do you typically take as a leader? How do you respond when feeling negative emotions such as anger, frustration or fear? To gain insight, use the four vulnerability tools for a month, keeping a log of what you're doing to break with your habitual behaviours as well as how your colleagues and peers are responding. At the end of the month, make a broad assessment about the tone you typically project as a leader, and decide on some longer-term adjustments you might make to show more vulnerability.

Sixteen

Graduation Day

Remember Maggie, the doctor of physical therapy who struggled to appreciate her superpowers? She was so entangled in negative narratives about herself that she undercharged clients and worked longer hours than she wanted to for fear of disappointing them. By using "I Am Powerful" in conjunction with the other tools, she weaned herself off those narratives and overpowered her Devil, deeply internalizing a sense of self-worth. She developed the courage she needed to raise her prices, set boundaries for clients and take the time she needed to nourish herself.

Maggie began moving toward her 25th hour almost immediately by using the tools, but it took her time to master them and embed them deeply. A turning point came about a year into our work together. Not only was she routinely carving out a 25th hour for herself; she had mustered the strength to finally have a series of difficult but necessary conversations about her pricing with longtime clients. Afterward, it became clear to both of us that she hadn't simply made incremental changes but had engineered what she calls a "pivotal shift" in her life.

We couldn't let that moment pass, so I introduced Maggie to a tool called "Graduation Day" in which you formally "graduate" from the course of work contained in this book. While most graduation ceremonies take place in public with friends and loved ones in attendance, this one is just for you. Standing alone before a mirror, you give a short speech describing your accomplishments and what they've meant to you. Including a bit of ritual helps make this moment special; Maggie put on the beautiful sash she'd worn when she'd received her doctorate, symbolizing the end of one chapter of her life and the beginning of a new period of growth and discovery. She doesn't remember exactly what she said in her speech, but she does know that she expressed pride in and gratitude for all she'd accomplished. As she recalled, the ceremony was "simple, quiet, and profoundly empowering".

I first thought of "Graduation Day" a decade ago while attending my oldest son's high school graduation. As I watched Jordan walk across the stage to receive his degree, it struck me that the ceremony was such a powerful marker of all the passion he'd put into his studies and the personal growth he'd experienced. It also served as a launchpad for all he *would* do, sending him on his next adventure with a boost of positive energy.

Some of my clients were in a position very much like Jordan's. They'd worked enormously hard learning the tools and seen tremendous growth, moving from conflict, drama, anxiety and self-doubt to a more positive way of being. They'd learned to be more courageous, to believe in themselves more, to tolerate more discomfort and to change entrenched habits that were hurting them. That was just the beginning of what they would accomplish as they continued to master and deploy their tools. Wouldn't it be great, I thought, if I created an exercise that would help them acknowledge their progress and inspire them to continue? Wouldn't it be great if the tool also gave them a bit of structure for pursuing their ongoing work?

Marking Your Passage

To perform "Graduation Day", first confirm that you've met my strict criteria for graduating. Look back at your "Credits and Debits" notebook and tally up the days when you earned a 25th hour. For each week you worked with your tools and earned a 25th hour on five consecutive days, give yourself a credit. If you've amassed twenty credits, you've met one requirement for graduation. But there's a second: like Maggie, you also must document a perceptible improvement in your external circumstances thanks to your ability to manage yourself. This could be a dramatically improved relationship, the resolution of a long-standing conflict, an important change you've made in your life, or specific life or career challenges that you surmounted. Many of my clients take at least a year to get to this point, while some require several years. Some never get there – and that's okay. We all go at our own pace.

If you're ready to graduate, mark time in your calendar for your ceremony, locate or buy a cap and gown, and start thinking about the speech you're going to give yourself that day. Wearing a cap and gown or other ritual garments is corny for sure, yet they add levity while also reminding us of the exercise's importance. Regardless of what you wear, the real work here is to look in the mirror on graduation day and give yourself credit for all that you've accomplished and will continue to accomplish while working with the tools. You can then give yourself a little reward by celebrating the milestone, going out to your favourite restaurant or doing something else that you enjoy.

To get a better sense of what a graduation day speech might look like, consider another client of mine, Samantha. When I first met her, she was miserable in her role as a human resources executive at a public company, plagued by a boss who was needy, mercurial, insensitive and impossible to please. He'd think nothing of calling up his team on a Sunday afternoon and demanding that they jump online immediately for a meeting to hear about some harebrained idea that had come to him. He verbally abused his team members, complaining about how terrible they were at their jobs. The irony was that he frequently underperformed himself, leaving Samantha to pick up the pieces. Over time, she took on the role of mother hen, ministering to team members who came to her upset and needing to vent. All the time she spent handling her destructive boss bogged her down and left her feeling overwhelmed and burned out.

When she began using the tools, especially "What's the Intent?" and "Ask Clarifying Questions", she shrank the thirty- or forty-five-minute venting sessions she was having each day with team members down to five minutes. As she mastered the tools, she became more courageous and confident in her abilities. She began erecting boundaries between herself and the CEO, which helped make her job more manageable. After about eighteen months, her stronger sense of self led her to finally say goodbye to her boss altogether. Leaving the company, she opened her own firm, consulting with companies around HR issues and opportunities. Within eighteen months, she was making more money than she had before while enjoying more independence and a better work-life balance.

I don't know exactly what Samantha said during her "Graduation Day" exercise, but I'm pretty sure it went something like this: "Wow, what a journey this has been. I started out as a reasonably successful HR professional with a major case of the Ucks, and now I'm running my own business. I've used my tools to develop not just myself but others around me, helping them find their 25th hour. It wasn't easy: I went through all kinds of ups and downs as I learned how to manage myself. Laying down boundaries with my boss wasn't easy, either. But it's so satisfying being able to handle a conversation in just five minutes that used to take thirty. And using 'What's the Intent?' has helped me avoid negative feelings. I'm now spreading positivity instead of negative vibes. And I plan to continue doing that far into the future. I want to continue to be a dynamic professional while finding even more ways to nurture myself. I want to feel an even deeper belief in myself and all that I have to offer the world."

Writing a graduation day speech for yourself affords you a unique opportunity to pause and reflect on where you've been, the hard work you've done and the growth that has resulted. You might decide to perform "Ten Minutes a Day" each day for a week, using that time of quiet and solitude to think back on what you've done in recent months. Or set aside a longer block of time – an hour or two – to think and reflect. How have you used the tools? What unproductive habits have you changed? How have you reprogrammed your robot and tamed your Devil? What epiphanies have you experienced about yourself? At what key moments did you break free from mediocrity to become truly Exceptional? How has your work with the tools impacted your life? What can you do and enjoy now, thanks to your ability to manage yourself better, that was once inaccessible to you? How have your relationships and your health changed? Reflect, too, on areas that need work: what kinds of situations continue to trip you up? What other bad habits might you address? What relationships do you hope to improve in the months ahead? What do you feel is still holding you back?

As clarifying as it can be to craft a graduation day speech, it's just as helpful to deliver it to yourself before a mirror. As you saw with a tool such as "I Am Powerful", it's empowering to look yourself in the eye and give yourself an affirmative, positive message. Articulating the words out loud crystallizes the message in your mind, giving it more weight. Doing so also serves as a powerful expression of your emotional maturity. Just as we can't expect the outside world to understand and appreciate our unique powers, we can't expect it to mark all that we've accomplished on our growth path. Affirming and celebrating our *own* growth is yet another part of what it means to manage our own emotions. We're acknowledging our own emotional needs and providing for them rather than placing the burden on others.

This observation brings me to a final but critically important part of "Graduation Day". When we marched across the stage at our high school or college graduation, other people showered gifts on us. This time, we must give ourselves gifts. There's one in particular that I have in mind. Buy yourself a notebook and designate it as your 25th Hour Logbook. Each day after your graduation, record how you used the extra time that the effective use of your tools has created for you. Note the meaning that the activity had for you. If you used the time to attend your kid's sporting event or to exercise, write it down and note how it enriched your life. Did it bring you closer to your child? Did it make you feel as though you were being the parent you had always dreamed of being?

Some clients of mine continue this new practice of logging their 25th hour indefinitely. As time passes, you might go back to chapters of this book for a refresh, updating or customizing the tools in ways that you find helpful and natural. As I think you'll find, recording these small daily wins will keep you motivated to continue by making you aware of the benefits you're seeing. It will also remind you that managing yourself requires ongoing work and commitment. On days when you slip and either didn't earn time or lost it, make a quick note about what happened and how you plan to handle similar situations differently going forward. Don't get down on yourself. As I've suggested throughout this book, the point isn't to achieve perfection. You *will* slip up. But you'll do so less often, and you'll recover more quickly, laughing at how ridiculously you're behaving and moving on.

Steadier on Your Feet

On a deeper level, I've found that graduation day marks the start of a new phase of stability in my clients' lives. When my clients first come to me, they have many of the ingredients they need to succeed. They know how to work hard and achieve. They're smart, talented, committed people. But since they lack the ability to handle their emotional responses, they find themselves constantly veering off track. Upon reaching graduation day, they've found that their ability to manage themselves has made life smoother and more stable, enabling them to focus on their priorities and achieve more. They become their own emotional rock in the storm, and they also serve that function for others. In some cases, this sense of stability helps my clients weather extreme circumstances they never thought they'd encounter.

In chapter 5, I told you about Ellie, a highly successful CFO who used "It's My Fault" to improve her fraught relationship with Nikki, her company's head of human resources. That was a major achievement, dramatically improving her work environment and leading to performance gains for the entire company. Combined with all the time Ellie was saving by using her other tools, her ability to heal her relationship with Nikki and avoid further drama no doubt qualified her to participate in the "Graduation Day" exercise.

What neither Ellie nor I realized was that her ability to manage her emotions would soon be tested as never before by a tragedy in her personal life. When Ellie and I had worked together for about eighteen months, her husband received a devastating cancer diagnosis. He passed away about six weeks later. For the next year or so, Ellie struggled with intense grief. The tools didn't save her from pain and suffering, but as she attested, they helped a great deal. As she explained, "When you're grieving, you're not thinking about somebody else's feelings at that point. You're just like, 'You guys, I'm going to show up today and that's the best that I can do today, but I'll show up and do the best that I can.'" By using the tools, Ellie at least had some strategies that she could fall back on to prevent her from reacting and perseverating. She could use them "to focus in on how I get through the day, knowing that one day I'm going to want to show back up and continue to work here."

At one point about two months into the grieving process, when

Ellie was back at work, her CEO approached to complain about something she hadn't done to his liking. Her first impulse was to stand her ground and speak her truth. "I know life has moved on for you," she told her boss, "but it hasn't for my family. I am giving you everything I have. And I need you to show me some compassion while I work through this." As Ellie reflected, a reaction like that "is something that I never would have done" before working with the tools. Either she would have stayed quiet, refraining from setting a reasonable boundary with her boss, or she would have quit out of frustration at being pushed too hard at a delicate time. Because she'd used the tools, she was able to step outside her emotions while also mustering the courage to communicate her needs. Rather than sparking drama, she addressed the problem directly with her boss. He understood her situation and responded compassionately by backing off, giving her the "time and space to heal" that she required.

Ellie didn't always use her tools well. Sometimes her pain was just too intense, and she found herself falling back on old habits. "But I always had the toolbox to reach into," she said. The tools and the thinking behind them had become so ingrained that "I had a good enough foundation to pull on those tools when I really, really needed them." Looking back on it, Ellie suspects that the loss of her husband even helped strengthen her use of the tools, particularly those related to vulnerability. A trauma like that "forces you to be vulnerable", she said, precisely because she felt so broken inside. She found it easier than she had before to overcome her fear and express herself to those around her.

More broadly, grieving led her to become more deliberate about her behaviour and more determined to behave in alignment with her ideals. She found herself using her tools intensively to scrutinize her responses to situations and determine whether her emotions were interceding. "Pause Button" helped here, giving her that little bit of space she needed to step outside her emotional response and look at a situation more objectively. "Ask Clarifying Questions" helped her, too, by enabling her to approach business meetings from a position of curiosity rather than judgment or anger. And "Gratitude Equals Joy" helped her by enabling her to step away from anger and petty resentments and find the joy in difficult situations. Rather than reacting to perceived slights, she took a more empathic and compassionate view, allowing her rational self more space to identify and solve the underlying problems.

When Ellie failed to use her tools properly, she didn't get down about it. We playfully labelled such moments "Ellie 1.0", as compared with her new, more emotionally mature self, which she labelled "Ellie 2.0". She acknowledged her missteps, asked herself what she might learn from them, and recommitted herself to using the tools. "Me beating myself up only sets me back," she said, "and I've worked way too hard to get to where I am to become my own worst enemy."

Ellie reported that the experience of losing her husband made the time she saved by managing herself seem more precious to her. She felt motivated to do more to achieve it, including by taking unorthodox approaches to solving problems. "We're so used to the grind and busting down the wall that now I see the value in sometimes I'm going to walk around the wall, sometimes I'm going to walk over the wall, sometimes I'm going to chip away at the wall. I'll see what the situation calls for, and I'm going to take the path that inspires and gives me back my 25th hour." Time, she reflects, is truly a gift we're given, and as she knows all too well, it's a limited resource. We must be more deliberate in using it, asking ourselves, "What am I going to do with it every single day?"

All of us will experience pain, suffering and disappointment. We can't control what happens to us, but we can control how we respond. I hope that the sense of stability you gain by using the tools will enable you to become more resilient during the hard times. I hope it will help you learn what you can from adversity and, like Ellie, come through it even stronger. In ways we don't always recognize, our Ordinary behaviour depletes us, causing our time to feel insufficient and stressful. But we have it in our power to fix the situation. So put down this book and get started. With a bit of effort and focus, you'll move toward your own "Graduation Day", perhaps more quickly than you imagine. Your life will never be the same.

Find Your 25th Hour: Start with the Tools

It's well and good to read about the tools and the difference they can make. But change comes only if you use them. If you haven't yet started experimenting and practising, now is the time to start. Pick a tool from this book that resonates with you, and put it into use at least once over the next twenty-four hours. Afterward, reflect on the experience. Did it work for you? Why or why not? Keep practising the tool until you feel you've mastered it. Then try another. Don't feel that you need to go in order chapter by chapter. Skip around the book if you like, picking tools to work on that you feel most speak to the situations you're in and the struggles you're experiencing.

Epilogue

In the fall of 2021, after our youngest son, Drew, had begun his freshman year at a big midwestern university, my wife and I along with our oldest son, Jordan, visited for parents' weekend and to take in a football game together. I was still getting used to being an empty nester, so I was excited to see Drew and find out how he was adapting. What I didn't expect, amid the boisterous crowds of students, parents and alumni hyped up for the big game, was that I'd gain new insight into what it means to master emotions and achieve a more mature, elevated way of living.

On the Saturday evening of that weekend, we planned to enjoy a family dinner at a nice restaurant and then head to a rooftop bar for a casual gathering of first-year students and their parents. The weather that weekend was unusually hot and sticky. By Saturday afternoon, Drew's T-shirt and shorts were filthy from his daily routine. We expected that he'd clean himself up before the evening's festivities, but he had other ideas. When he showed up at the restaurant, he was wearing the same dirty clothes. Worse, he'd also put on a ratty old flannel pyjama top that had been on our short list of garments to give to Goodwill but that he'd claimed for himself while packing for college.

My first sight of Drew triggered me (I mean, what the heck!), but I quickly moved past that, reflecting how I'd been as an eighteen-year-old boy. Beth, meanwhile, shot Drew a look and said, "What's happening? This is a nice restaurant! You were supposed to have showered and cleaned yourself up."

"I did shower," he said. "I just put the same clothes back on."

Ordinary in our thinking, Beth and I wondered aloud if that was how Drew had been presenting himself so far in class and to his new dormmates and friends. We asked if he wanted to change his outfit, given that we were meeting up with several of the parents and kids after dinner. Wasn't he worried that he'd stick out?

He waved us off. "It'll be fine."

We enjoyed our dinner and then went to the rooftop bar to socialize. It turned out that Beth and I were right about the impact of Drew's unconventional fashion choices. He did stick out from the other students. But not in the way either of us expected. When we entered the rooftop area, something crazy happened. A portion of the party in progress suddenly reorganized itself around Drew. Several kids shouted "Drew!" and flocked to greet him. Other kids who were clustered around said to one another, "Oh, look, Drew's here, let's go talk to him, let's meet his parents!" For the next half hour, Drew became the hub of the scene as student after student came over to say hello and introduce their parents to him and us. I'd never seen anything like it. You would have thought Drew was a rock star – that was the kind of greeting he received. Bear in mind, Drew had known those kids for only a few weeks. Clearly he'd made a huge impression.

Watching Drew chatting with his new friends, I turned to Jordan and remarked on all the attention Drew was receiving. How could that be happening? As Jordan shared his impressions, I came to understand the situation a bit better. It wasn't just that Drew was a gregarious, friendly, likeable kid; on a deeper level, what attracted his peers to him so powerfully was *his obvious and profound comfort in his own skin*. Drew didn't feel compelled to conform to the expectations of others, whether about how he dressed, what he said in conversation or anything else. He wasn't trying to impress people or manage their impressions of him. Life for him was simpler than that. He intuitively understood that it was okay for him just to be himself. That, coupled with his uncanny awareness of his emotions, enabled him to shine and move smoothly through the room – and his life. His superpower, I concluded, was his ability to behave in ways that were fundamentally Exceptional.

It might surprise you to hear me say this about a teenage boy, but I'd long thought of Drew as one of the most Exceptional people I knew. Maybe it was growing up around my tools or maybe it was that he was the youngest child and learned from his older brothers. But whatever it was, behaving in an Exceptional way just seemed natural and intuitive to him. *Of course* he thought about *why* people act or speak as they do. *Of course* he asked questions of people to tease out their intentions before jumping to conclusions. *Of course* he celebrated his successes and reminded himself of his own power. *Of course* he took steps to yank himself away from his emotions when they ran amok. *Of course* he took responsibility for his own performance when working on a team. *Of course* he made himself vulnerable around others instead of trying to be perfect. And on and on.

Drew was so uniquely good at behaving Exceptionally that he often helped *me* when I was veering off track. In fact, he still does. As I was editing this book, I had a disappointing professional encounter that despite all of my knowledge, teachings and practice sent me swirling. For a good three days, I couldn't shut off the intrusive thoughts I was having about how an associate of mine had treated me. My 25th hour was shot to hell. Drew came home one evening and saw me swirling. When I explained the situation, he said, "Dad, don't you teach this to others all day long? We live Exceptionally. Why would you let this person's shenanigans get to you? You're constantly managing other people's situations. Use your tools and just turn it off."

He went on to say that if he were in my position, he'd tell himself that the other person's actions made no sense and were *their* problem. Reminding himself of the deep respect he'd earned from others within the company and beyond, he'd realize that thinking any more about the situation was a waste of time. Boom – he'd move on. His advice that day prompted me to use my tools to pull myself out of my negative thinking and swirl so that I could move on without wasting any more time.

Drew's example points us to the inner growth that can occur if we aim for a 25th hour over time: we not only achieve the kind of stability and calmness I described in chapter 16, we also come to *see life differently*. We move through the world with poise and confidence, attracting others into our orbit without even trying. We take ownership of our lives and our emotional experiences. We accept ourselves wholeheartedly and without reservation, both the good stuff and the areas where we could stand to improve. If that means dressing down when everyone else is dressing up, great!

All of us have looked at people who appear unusually strong and self-possessed and wondered, *How do they do it? What's the secret to living life so smoothly and simply?* Now you know. These aren't eccentric or unique personalities. Rather, they're people for whom Exceptional ways of behaving have become ingrained and automatic, either because they grew up that way or because they worked on themselves over a period of time.

When you find such people, hold them close, even if they're younger or less experienced than you. Watch them carefully, and allow yourself to be astonished. Learn from them, as I try to do not only with Drew but with each of my kids, embracing their unique individuality. Invite them to give you feedback, so that you can move your own practice forward.

I have one last exercise for you, one that I like to call "My Dream Life". Think about someone you know who moves through the world as Drew does. Ask yourself: what would my life be like if I completely owned my actions rather than following the herd? Envision a life filled with Exceptional behaviours and opportunities. How fulfilling would your daily experiences be? What kinds of behaviours would you adopt? Take ten minutes to really think it through. And then, using the tools in this book, start making those dreams a reality.

I wish you every success!

Acknowledgments

I mentioned that this book began with encouragement I received from various clients of mine. One of them, Lorenzo, went so far as to make introductions on my behalf. So allow me to begin these acknowledgments by thanking him for not just motivating me to pursue this project but giving me an important kick in the butt.

Next, it's a great pleasure to thank those who helped directly with this project. To my writing partner, Seth Schulman: Wow! You are Exceptional! You made this process safe and simple and captured my voice better than I could have imagined. Thank you so much! I'm hugely grateful to my agents, Christy Fletcher and Sarah Fuentes, who along with the team at Simon & Schuster made this process simple and fun. A big thank-you for helping me develop my confidence as an author. You are true professionals, and I appreciate you.

I often say that I feel grateful for my "village" of loving family and friends, and that's absolutely true. First and foremost, I must thank my parents, who modelled community for me. Although I didn't understand it at the time, the independence they allowed me during my childhood helped shape me into the man I am today. I love and miss you both every day.

At the heart of my village is my wife, Beth. We met when we were twelve years old and started dating at fourteen. Thank you for loving me unconditionally and allowing me to love you back. You are my everything! We've created a magical and adventurous life together, and I am grateful beyond words for you!

To Jordan, Jared and Drew, my amazing and talented sons, you continuously inspire and challenge me. I'm so proud of the kind, ambitious, warm men you've become. I love learning from you and applaud you for pushing me out of my comfort zone. Thank you, Jordan and Jared, for bringing my brilliant and incredible daughters-in-law, Gabrielle and Tess, into my life. I love all of you endlessly, and you are the true prides and joys of my life.

To my sister, Andrea, thank you for helping me make sense of my childhood and for your wisdom and love. I will be forever grateful for all of your encouragement and guidance over the years. Also, to Beverly Stone, my second mom. Words can't express how much I appreciate the inspiration and professional role modelling you've given me.

I feel deeply grateful for the support of my YPO Forums and the deep connections and friendships we share. There's no way I would have pursued this book without your encouragement. Thank you for all of your direct and consistent feedback. Seriously, you seem to know me better than I know myself!

I am blessed with many friends who are like family. All of you know who you are. Thank you for your hugs, love and support. I adore you and your families and love our village beyond words.

To my first bosses at Interep, Jeff, Peter and Tom, thank you for allowing me to be me early in my career and for investing in my professional development. Because of you, I learned very early to start with trust instead of making my team work too hard to earn it.

To my Triton Digital Team, you truly are the best of the best. You taught me about cultural nuances and how to be a CEO as we navigated challenges and obstacles. You allowed me to teach and learn at the same time, and I am so proud of what we built. I am grateful for the opportunity to assemble and work with such a wonderful team.

To my Triton Digital CFO, Mark, who unfortunately passed away a few years ago: it was an honour to work with you and an even bigger honour to be your friend. We talked often about our second act together, and I'm sad that we're not able to pursue it. I think of you daily and miss you terribly.

I wish to express my gratitude as well to Jana for everything she's done to support me and my professional endeavours. You've become family to me and I'm truly blessed to have you aboard the team. You get me, and that isn't always simple.

To the 25th Hour Group Team, thank you for your support during this process. The "party" is just about to get started and we have lots of important work to do. Cheers to many years of helping countless professionals change their lives for the better. I can't think of anyone else I'd want by my side as we build this company.

I dedicate this book to my incredible, diverse and truly remarkable clients. I'm so grateful for the trust you continue to show in me and my toolbox. Remember, it's about *you* managing *you*, and since it's your fault anyway, you might as well make it simple, have fun and enjoy your 25th hour.

My heart is full, and I'm fired up by the work we do. Let's go!

Notes

One: The One Question You Can't Forget to Ask

1. Michael Tomasello et al., "Understanding and Sharing Intentions: The Origins of Cultural Cognition", *Behavioral and Brain Sciences* 28 (2005): 675–735, https://www.eva.mpg.de/documents/Cambridge/Boesch_Joint_BehBrainSci_2005_1555289.pdf.
2. Jason Hreha, "What Is Intentionality Bias in Behavioral Economics?", 2023, https://www.thebehavioralscientist.com/glossary/intentionality-bias.
3. For more on the science of emotional contagion, see Carolina Herrando and Efthymios Constantinides, "Emotional Contagion: A Brief Overview and Future Directions", *Frontiers in Psychology*, 15 July 2021, https://www.frontiersin.org/journals/psychology/articles/10.3389/fpsyg.2021.712606/full.
4. Sandra L Robinson and Kira Schabram, "When You're the Person Your Colleagues Always Vent To", *Harvard Business Review*, 30 November 2016, https://hbr.org/2016/11/when-youre-the-person-your-colleagues-always-vent-to. The authors define a toxic handler as "someone who voluntarily shoulders the sadness, frustration, bitterness and anger that are endemic to organizational life just as joy and success are."
5. Marshall Goldsmith, "Reducing Negativity in the Workplace", *Harvard Business Review*, 7 October 2007 https://hbr.org/2007/10/reducing-negativity-in-the-wor.

Two: How to Stop Yourself from Saying the Wrong Thing

1. Melanie Letendre Jauniaux and Heather L Lawford, "Interpersonal Curiosity as a Tool to Foster Safe Relational Spaces: A Narrative Literature Review", *Frontiers in Psychology*, 12 August 2024, https://www.frontiersin.org/journals/psychology/articles/10.3389/fpsyg.2024.1379330/full.
2. Todd B Kashdan et al., "Curiosity Protects Against Interpersonal Aggression: Cross-Sectional, Daily Process, and Behavioral Evidence",

Journal of Personality 81, no. 1 (2013): 87–102, https://doi.org/10.1111/j.1467-6494.2012.00783.x.

3. Spencer Harrison, Erin Pinkus and Jon Cohen, "Research: 83% of Executives Say They Encourage Curiosity. Just 52% of Employees Agree", *Harvard Business Review*, 20 September 2018, https://hbr.org/2018/09/research-83-of-executives-say-they-encourage-curiosity-just-52-of-employees-agree.
4. Alison Wood Brooks and Leslie K John, "The Surprising Power of Questions", *Harvard Business Review*, May–June 2018, https://hbr.org/2018/05/the-surprising-power-of-questions.

Three: Time Management as a Pathway to Personal Growth

1. Leslie A Perlow, Constance Noonan and Eunice Eun, "Stop the Meeting Madness", *Harvard Business Review*, July–August 2017, https://hbr.org/2017/07/stop-the-meeting-madness.
2. "The Cost of Meeting Attendance", Otter.ai, https://20067454.fs1.hubspotusercontent-na1.net/hubfs/20067454/Report_The%20Cost%20of%20Unnecessary%20Meeting%20Attendance.pdf.
3. "Will AI Fix Work?", Microsoft, 9 May 2023, https://www.microsoft.com/en-us/worklab/work-trend-index/will-ai-fix-work.

Four: The Simple Act of Slowing Down

1. Taylor Wendt, "Amygdala: What to Know", WebMD, 19 November 2024, https://www.webmd.com/brain/amygdala-what-to-know; Helen Owton, "The Amygdala Hijack: Stress Response in Aviation", OpenLearn, 5 June 2023, https://www.open.edu/openlearn/health-sports-psychology/the-amygdala-hijack-stress-response-aviation; Adaora Ayoade, "Strategies for Preventing Emotional Hijack at Work", *Forbes*, 28 June 2022, https://www.forbes.com/councils/forbescoachescouncil/2022/06/28/strategies-for-preventing-emotional-hijack-at-work; "Amygdala Neuron", ScienceDirect, https://www.sciencedirect.com/topics/medicine-and-dentistry/amygdala-neuron.
2. There are many visualization techniques, and some of them have been shown scientifically to afford these benefits. In one variant, called guided imagery, you imagine some positive situation that will occur in the future. Research has linked guided imagery with reduced pain, anxiety and other benefits. See, e.g., Stephen D Krau, "The Multiple Uses of Guided Imagery", *Nursing Clinics of North America* 55, no. 4 (2020): 467–74, https://doi.org/10.1016/j.cnur.2020.06.013.

Five: Make Everything Your Fault

1. Arlin Cuncic, "What Is Defensiveness?", Verywell Mind, 25 September 2025, https://www.verywellmind.com/what-is-defensiveness-5115075; Seth Meyers, "Why Some People Are So Defensive", *Psychology Today*, 28 September 2021, https://www.psychologytoday.com/intl/blog/insight-is-2020/202109/why-some-people-are-so-defensive.
2. Glen H Stamp, Anita L Vangelisti and John A Daly, "The Creation of Defensiveness in Social Interaction", *Communication Quarterly* 40, no. 2 (1992): 177–90, https://www.researchgate.net/profile/John-Daly-6/publication/241716171_The_Creation_of_Defensiveness_in_Social_Interaction/links/5626225708aed3d3f137e683/The-Creation-of-Defensiveness-in-Social-Interaction.pdf.
3. Ellie Lisitsa, "The Four Horsemen: Criticism, Contempt, Defensiveness, and Stonewalling", 15 October 2024, The Gottman Institute, https://www.gottman.com/blog/the-four-horsemen-recognizing-criticism-contempt-defensiveness-and-stonewalling.

Six: Turn Insults into Fuel

1. Allah D Wright, "What HR Can Do About Cyberbullying in the Workplace", SHRM, 13 May 2016, https://www.shrm.org/topics-tools/news/technology/hr-can-cyberbullying-workplace.
2. "What Are the Consequences of Incivility?", Hawai'i Community College, https://hawaii.hawaii.edu/civility/consequences-of-incivility.
3. Christine Porath and Christine Pearson, "The Price of Incivility", *Harvard Business Review*, January–February 2013, https://hbr.org/2013/01/the-price-of-incivility.
4. Clare Watson, "Spoken Insults Stir Up More Brain Activity than Compliments and Linger for Longer, Too", Science Alert, 4 September 2022, https://www.sciencealert.com/spoken-insults-stir-up-more-brain-activity-than-compliments-and-linger-for-longer-too.
5. Suzanna Burgelman, "Verbal Insults Trigger a 'Mini Slap to the Face,' Finds New Research", Frontiers, 18 July 2022, https://www.frontiersin.org/news/2022/07/18/verbal-insults-trigger-a-mini-slap-to-the-face-finds-new-research.
6. Rachel Hatch, "Research Shows Small Insults Have Large Impacts", Illinois State University, 4 February 2018, https://news.illinoisstate.edu/2018/02/research-shows-small-insults-large-impact.
7. Heather C Lench et al., "Anger Has Benefits for Attaining Goals", *Journal of Personality and Social Psychology* 126, no. 4 (2023): 587–602, https://doi.org/10.1037/pspa0000350.

8. Hilary Jacobs Hendel, "Ignoring Your Emotions Is Bad for Your Health. Here's What to Do About It", *Time*, 27 February 2018, https://time.com/5163576/ignoring-your-emotions-bad-for-your-health.

Seven: When You're Suffering from a Case of the Ucks, Do This

1. "Giving Thanks Can Make You Healthier", Harvard Health Publishing, 14 August 2021, https://www.health.harvard.edu/healthbeat/giving-thanks-can-make-you-happier.
2. Ashley J Smith, "Gratitude—A Mental Health Game Changer", Anxiety & Depression Association of America, 22 November 2023, https://adaa.org/learn-from-us/from-the-experts/blog-posts/consumer/gratitude-mental-health-game-changer.
3. Joshua Brown and Joel Wang, "How Gratitude Changes You and Your Brain", *Greater Good Magazine*, 6 June 2017, https://greatergood.berkeley.edu/article/item/how_gratitude_changes_you_and_your_brain.

Nine: Three Essential Tools for Confronting Your Fears

1. Dexter Tilo, "Fear Factor: Employees Reveal Deepest Workplace Phobias", Human Resources Director, 22 June 2023, https://www.hcamag.com/us/specialization/mental-health/fear-factor-employees-reveal-deepest-workplace-phobias/450558.
2. "Zety Survey Finds More than Half of Workers Claim Getting Fired Scares Them 'More than Death'", HRO Today, 26 June 2023, https://www.hrotoday.com/news/ticker/zety-survey-finds-more-than-half-of-workers-claim-getting-fired-scares-them-more-than-death.

Eleven: You're Powerful, and You Don't Even Know It!

1. According to a school of thought called "Self-Determination Theory", humans have a basic need to feel connection with others, and this need motivates their behaviour. See, e.g., Kirsten Weir, "Self-Determination Theory: A Quarter Century of Human Motivation Research", American Psychological Association, 2 March 2025, https://www.apa.org/research-practice/conduct-research/self-determination-theory.
2. Catherine Moore, "Positive Daily Affirmations: Is There Science Behind It?", PositivePsychology.com, 4 March 2019, https://positivepsychology.com/daily-affirmations; Daniel J Lannin et al., "How Is Spontaneous Self-Affirmation Linked to Self-Esteem? A Cross-Lagged Examination", *Journal of Research in Personality* 92 (2021): 104091, https://doi.org/10.1016/j.jrp.2021.104091.

Twelve: Give Yourself the Gift of Cookies

1. Sarah DiGiulio, "Why Compliments Make Us Feel So Good—And How to Get Better at Giving Them", Better by Today, 7 October 2019, https://www.nbcnews.com/better/lifestyle/why-compliments-make-us-feel-so-good-how-get-better-ncna1062546.
2. Erica J Boothby and Vanessa K Bohns, "Why a Simple Act of Kindness Is Not as Simple as It Seems: Underestimating the Positive Impact of Our Compliments on Others", *Personality and Social Psychology Bulletin* 47, no. 5 (2021): 826–40, https://doi.org/10.1177/0146167220949003.
3. Arthur C Brooks, "A Compliment That Really Means Something", *Atlantic*, 15 August 2024, https://www.theatlantic.com/ideas/archive/2024/08/give-great-compliment-happiness/679447.

Fourteen: Trust Yourself So That You Can Trust and Lead Others

1. David Finkel, "New Study Shows You're Wasting 21.8 Hours a Week", *Inc.*, 1 March 2018, https://www.inc.com/david-finkel/new-study-shows-youre-wasting-218-hours-a-week.html/.

Fifteen: Nurture Vulnerability

1. Brown's TED talk "The Power of Vulnerability" has been viewed almost 24 million times as of this writing in June 2025. See TED, *The Power of Vulnerability | Brené Brown | TED*, YouTube, 3 January 2011, https://www.youtube.com/watch?v=iCvmsMzlF7o. A transcript of this talk is available at https://fs.blog/great-talks/power-vulnerability-brene-brown. See also her book *Daring Greatly: How the Courage to Be Vulnerable Transforms the Way We Live, Love, Parent, and Lead* (Avery, 2012).

Index

About the Author

Neal Schore serves as chairman and adviser to several notable business leaders, boards and companies across the United States. He also advises multiple private equity and investment firms on executive leadership and strategic initiatives. He currently serves as cofounder and CEO of the 25th Hour Group, an executive coaching and leadership events firm that showcases his proven leadership toolbox and practice. Previously, Schore served as founder, president and CEO of Triton Digital, a global technology, data and services leader in the digital audio and podcast industry. Schore received a bachelor of arts in business administration, with emphasis on management, marketing and finance, from Michigan State University. He is currently active in Harvard Business School's Executive Education programme. Schore is a member of the Los Angeles Gold Southland Chapter of the Young Presidents Organization (YPO) and recipient of Ernst & Young's 2011 Entrepreneur Of The Year award for Greater Los Angeles.